Just Along for the Ride

THE MISSIONARY JOURNEY OF PASTOR MARC AND NANCY ERICKSON

Deborah Wenzler Farris

Narrative Nonfiction

Ten|16
PRESS

Published by Ten16 Press, an imprint of Orange Hat Publishing

For information, please contact:
www.orangehatpublishing.com
Wauwatosa, WI

"To every man there openeth A way,
and ways, and a way.
And the high soul climbs the high way,
And the low soul gropes the low:
And in between, on the misty flats,
The rest drift to and fro.
But to every man there openeth
A high way and a low,
And every man must choose.
The way his soul shall go."

— John Oxenham

Table of Contents

Foreword

By Matt and Kelly Erickson

Sitting on the desk in my office is a track and field baton with these words etched into it:

"As I was with Moses, so I will be with you; I will never leave you nor forsake you. Be strong and courageous, because you will lead these people to inherit the land I swore to their ancestors to give them." (Joshua 1:5-6)

It is a regular reminder of the challenge and responsibility to carry forward the legacy of ministry at Eastbrook Church, where I currently serve as Senior Pastor. Throughout our church's history, a strong sense of ministry and mission has been upheld by our entire church, but also by our founding pastoral couple, Dr. Marc and Nancy Erickson.

This book tells part of their story, reading in one way like a love story, in another way like an adventure novel, but most foundationally like the story of a man and woman giving themselves over to God as best as they could. From their beginnings as students with Marc in training to be a doctor, they were touched by God's heart for the world. And that theme continued until, in humility, they released ministry to the next generation with trust. This story is inspiring and important for our current moment.

There are few people we know personally who have lived so dynamically, generously, and sacrificially, always pointing others to Jesus as Marc and Nancy.

When we began discussing ministry with Marc, he told us many stories, some filled with joy and others depicting the cost of ministry. He reminded us of Jesus, the One upon whose life both Marc and Nancy were centered, the One whom they were obsessed with telling others about, whether in Somalia or Milwaukee.

We have learned so much from Marc and Nancy. We have learned about the importance of relationships with and learning from our brothers and sisters around the world. We have learned about prayer, whether communal prayer over the city, persevering prayer for the congregation, or sacrificial prayer for our international friends and partners. We have learned about humility and sacrifice—humility to take a beating and keep proclaiming Jesus' name and the sacrifice of leading a diverse and sometimes messy congregation.

We are personally thankful to God for the Chinese scholar that Marc and Nancy took into their home many years ago. That scholar's daughter became one of our closest friends, and an aunt to our three boys. God's faithfulness is never-ending, and He continues His blessings from one generation to the next.

We thank God for Marc and Nancy, who established a foundation at the church we now serve and who handed the baton of pastoral leadership to us with all humility and trust because of their faith in Jesus.

We hope and pray you enjoy reading this book as

much as we have, laughing out loud at times at the adventures and crying at times at the depths of God's goodness and glory in His servants.

May this story inspire us, as well, to take our place within the stories of faith that echo from Hebrews 11 around the world and into our own day.

Matt Erickson, Senior Pastor, and Kelly Erickson, Spiritual Director, Eastbrook Church

A Note from the Author

Stories are our precious gifts, never static, ever-unfolding, like us. We gather around a fire pit or a table or an altar, to listen, to share, and at the very least, we learn, we grow, we are never left unchanged. But also in the telling and retelling of stories—of lives past, cultures gone by—we bring people and places and communities into the present that lead us into the future. The stories continue on through us.

At best, I've captured a glimpse of Marc and Nancy Erickson and the many incredible people that have been, and continue to be, a part of their lives in the United States and all around the world. Some of the names have been changed and others are simply referred to as "friend" in order to protect the individual's privacy. It's essential I note that many, many people who are important to Marc and Nancy and have played a significant role in their lives, have not been mentioned by name at all. It would take many books to even begin to mention all the people involved and praying. So may the storytelling continue for each of us and live on for the next generation to pass on and on.

To all who have laughed and wept, prayed and danced, wrestled and celebrated with me through the journey of writing this book, I offer my deep gratitude, and hope you are honored in the chapters that follow.

Deborah Wenzler Farris

PART ONE

Where Are You?

CHAPTER 1

Chemistry Class

"Wherever you are, be all there! Live to the hilt every situation you believe to be the will of God."
— Jim Elliot

Wheaton College, Illinois 1960

She was the new girl, transferring from a university on a quarter system to one on a semester basis, which put her at a disadvantage. It was her first day, and she sat in chemistry lab with an open book in front of her. The problem she stared at was bigger than she had the ability to solve. The other students seemed so capable. She was a bright girl and loved solving problems. That wasn't the problem, and she loved being with people. She wasn't shy. Maybe just a little, but no one could bring people together more easily. Now here she sat, feeling isolated and lost.

Her stomach was in knots, and her eyes stung back tears, but she was determined to try. She sighed. Why had she transferred? She knew why, but today that didn't even seem real. At the moment, it felt like a dream. Why hadn't she stayed where she was, where she felt comfortable? She could go back. She thought about gathering up her things and leaving the book altogether. She could walk out the door and never look back, but instead, she looked up.

Across the table, she saw him and straightened up. Had he noticed her floundering, her self-assurance so shaken? He looked up just then, his eyes deep, soulful, and kind. Suddenly, her fear was gone—fear of inadequacy, of failure, of letting her parents down, of letting herself down, and even worse, of letting God down. Hadn't He led her here? As the young man's eyes met hers, a calm swept over her. She didn't have a clue what to do, but in a single moment, she rose and walked toward him. "Can you help me?" she asked.

The boy with the kind eyes whose name she didn't yet know nodded, and she slid onto the stool beside him, relief replacing defeat.

"Sure."

"Thank you." She whispered the words like a prayer. "Thank you," she repeated, this time to Him.

He wasn't surprised to be attracted to her. He shook his head as if he were trying to tell himself otherwise, but it seemed to him, she lit up the room.

He had just received a phone call before chemistry class that day and knew he was needed at home. He needed to return just after starting the new semester. So he had to focus, finish his work, and get going. He wasn't sure what the semester ahead would hold. He was a sophomore and had never really dated. This was by his decision. His heart was set on one thing: he wanted to work in missions overseas. He knew a Savior who had given him everything, and there were many people around the world he knew needed healing and hope. In fact, he was willing to go to the greatest extremes, to the furthest reaches, the darkest, most dangerous places to help heal bodies, to heal lives. And he would go with the One who could heal broken spirits, who could bring wholeness from within. The places he planned to go would not be safe for a woman or safe to raise a family. He was willing to give that all up. He could never expect a woman to do the same, and with determined intention, he had created a boundary.

He finished his computations quickly, confident he was ahead of schedule and had time to spare. Lifting his gaze to check the time, he saw her. He was aware of his heart as a muscular organ, pumping blood through the vessels of his circulatory system. He knew it carried oxygen and nutrients to his body, carbon dioxide to his lungs. It was generally about the size of his closed fist and located between his lungs, in the middle compartment of his chest, this he knew. But he didn't understand why that space was suddenly not sufficient to contain it. His heart gave him life, and he had given his life, his heart, to the One who had created his heart. What was this heart of his telling him in this single moment, when his eyes met hers, and the space in his chest wasn't large enough to contain the surge of emotion? He smiled. She smiled back.

He couldn't explain what he was experiencing within his heart at that moment. He'd never experienced it before; there was no explanation for what he felt as she stood in front of him. His eyes widened as he heard her voice. "Can you help me?"

The formulas were solved that day, and they both left the lab changed. They had experienced what some may call love at first sight. They weren't expecting it. They weren't looking for it, and yet it happened. But the next day, he wasn't sitting in his seat. Her heart dropped. Such elation one day, followed by such disappointment the next. The chaplain asked the students to pray for Marc Erickson. He told the student body that Marc had flown home to Seattle because his sister was dying. When his mother called, Marc told the chaplain he already knew it was about his sister and that she was dying. The chaplain asked how he knew, and Marc answered him. "God told me."

A week later, Marc returned to school and came in to pick up his mail. Nancy saw him again. He tutored her on the chemistry lesson that night in the lab. Nancy wanted to know about his sister. He told her she had suffered from diabetes since infancy and at age twenty-four she had lost her sight, but she still went to Bible school. "She was extraordinary." He told Nancy how much the whole family loved his sister, and then he asked her about her own family. They laughed that it was a funny way to get to know each other. They could see how much family and spiritual roots meant to each of them. They felt so drawn to each other so quickly. He got scared because he had already told the Lord he wanted to go places he couldn't take a family.

"I'm planning to go overseas to be a missionary, and I'm probably not going to live very long. I plan to go to places I could never take a wife." But many of Nancy's family members had been in missions, and they had left a huge impression on her. Her Uncle Paul had worked in the Congo as a doctor for forty years.

"I can do that," she said with spunk and a spark in her eye.

CHAPTER 2

Early Encounters with God

"It is not the healthy who need a doctor,
but the sick." (Luke 5:31, NIV)

Spokane, Washington 1949

Marc's early years took him from Bemidji, Minnesota, and from there to Little Rock, Arkansas, then to St. Cloud, Minnesota, and on to Spokane, Washington, Clinton, Iowa, Seattle, Washington, and many moves back and forth. By his own definition, he was a hellion through fourth grade, but in the same breath, he would add that most preacher's kids were. His mother, Delnora, knew he wasn't a believer and wasn't doing what he was supposed to be doing. She ran the Vacation Bible School at church and challenged the children to memorize Scripture by saying anyone who learned three hundred verses could go to camp for free. She gave Marc verses each year so he could attend for free, and he memorized them mostly because he liked the ping pong and cookies at camp. By the time he'd outgrown camp, he knew a thousand Bible verses, which stuck with him. He wasn't yet a believer, but he knew the words and would never forget them.

Delnora was a farmer's daughter with a pastor's heart.

She was a smart woman and loved to teach the Bible. She would go up and down the streets near their house in Seattle, knocking on doors, getting to know the women. Pretty soon, she had a class of twenty-five women who had no idea what life was about, meeting with her in her home. She sincerely enjoyed getting to know the families within a few miles. She knew more about what was going on in the area than the mayor did, and she had a special way of connecting to people and introducing them to Christ. What she enjoyed most was seeing how miraculously their lives would change.

When Marc was ten years old, a pastor came to town and preached a sermon on Paul that inspired him. Marc realized he wanted to be like Paul, but he was a scrawny little kid and nobody paid attention to him. After hearing the sermon that night, he went home and told his mother he had gone forward after the service to accept Christ, but nobody would talk to him. She told his father, Ralph, about it. Although Ralph could talk to anybody, for some reason, he couldn't talk to his own son about Christ. A month later, another guest speaker came and preached on Hell. That really motivated Marc to give his heart to Christ. He went rushing down the aisle to the platform, but again, no one talked to him. So Delnora said again, "Ralph, Marc went forward again tonight. You have to talk to him."

"Okay, okay," Ralph said.

But Marc sat in his room waiting and thinking, "He's not coming, Lord. It's just between you and me." So he went over the verses he knew, and John 3:16 stood out, "For God so loved the world." Marc told God he believed it was true and he gave his heart to Christ. When he climbed in bed that night, he knew he was a Christian.

There were several significant events that happened in Marc's life following that incident. One morning, his friend, Billy Pearson, came to the house to walk to school with him. The Erickson family read Scripture and prayed together every morning. That morning, Delnora grabbed Billy and pulled him inside. "We're just ready to read and pray. Come join us!"

Billy looked pretty uncomfortable at the table, but he prayed for the first time in his entire life. That week, his mother died. Up until then, Marc hadn't thought much about death, but this sobered him up. Billy lost hope after his mother died. Sitting on the swing set together one afternoon, Marc explained the Gospel to him. It was the first time he had ever shared it with anyone. He told Billy that he would see his mother again.

A year later, Marc made friends with a neighbor boy named Jerry Ball. They walked home from school each day together. That fall, Jerry kept acting stranger and stranger, and finally quit doing his homework. The kids warned Marc about Jerry's odd behavior and told him to stay away from him. Jerry was going around telling people that he worked for the Nazis and then would threaten to kill them. What had happened, though, was that at age twelve, Jerry had a schizophrenic break. Nobody understood it at the time or knew what to do about it. But Marc was able to get him to do his homework and became a hero with the teachers. No one knew what to do with Jerry, but he trusted Marc. It was the first time Marc had an experience with schizophrenia.

After school one day, they were playing chess and Marc explained the Gospel to Jerry. He prayed and Jerry received Christ. The very next day, Jerry was admitted to a psychiatric hospital and Marc never saw Jerry again. It set the tone for Marc that there was nothing certain in life. People died, and died unexpectedly. A relationship with Christ was important. When Jerry lost his mind, he realized losing your life wasn't the only thing to fear. You could lose your mind even at a young age, and lose your chance to turn to God. It put a sense of urgency in Marc's life that never left him. "It was a gift from God."

This was the atmosphere Marc grew up in. When the family made a move to Iowa, the first thing they did was find a church. "It was pretty obvious; no one in the church there believed much of anything." The best sermon they got was "a good face". Marc started going to the high school Sunday school class where there were about ten kids attending. The pastor got upset and told Marc that he was rocking the boat by "saying Jesus was who He said He was and sent His Holy Spirit to empower every believer." The pastor tried to straighten Marc out, but the kids didn't listen to him. The pastor seemed to know about Jesus, but he really didn't know Jesus. He didn't believe God was still able to do miracles through His followers. Marc started teaching, and the class grew to about forty kids. He was beginning to see he had a calling. The amazing part to Marc was, God had plans for him before he had plans for God. He had learned early from his father how important people are. If a person gives their life to Christ, they're going to live a life they won't be able to explain. He thought that was really exciting to see happen, and he knew in his heart, they were going to outlive the universe.

In Marc's sophomore year of high school, his family moved to Seattle. There, Marc helped his mother start a church. Seattle seemed to be a spiritual wasteland. Delnora had fun getting to know her new neighborhood. She often went door to door, inviting people to the new church. She started a high school youth group and had a special knack for introducing people to Christ and seeing their lives change. She had great stories that inspired Marc. His mother believed in him and felt he could do anything he set his mind to. She even bought him a suit and told him he looked like Billy Graham.

~

Marc's father, Ralph, was forty years old when Marc was born. It took Marc a long time to figure his father out. But Ralph had a strong influence on his son because of his love for people. Ralph may never have become important in the world's eyes, but that never bothered him. He helped people all the time. He had found Christ in his late twenties and he never looked back. His degree in history came from the University of Minnesota, where his professors counseled him to go to medical school, which is what they always counseled their brightest students. But instead, Ralph went to Bible

School and then on to seminary.

In his father's first pastorate, the church often didn't have the money to pay his salary. The Erickson family was so poor, at one point, Ralph began selling their furniture out of their home to feed his family. But a professor friend from Bible School found out about it and drove through the night, bought all the furniture, and gave it back to him. Ralph explained to Marc that what his friend did was a picture of authentic Christianity. At this point, Ralph became a chaplain with the Civilian Conservation Corp (CCC), a government job program during the Depression. He was always taking care of people, like Bob. Bob was an engineer, a builder, and a pastor, but times were hard. In the midst of it all, he was diagnosed with Multiple Sclerosis and had to leave his church.

Ralph knew how broken and useless Bob felt, and invited him and his wife to come and live with them. As Bob began to feel a bit stronger, Ralph suggested he build an addition on to their home. It would give Bob and his wife some space, and perhaps accomplishing something would help Bob feel good about himself again. So Bob added a big room onto the house. It did have quite a few quirks—a half step down here, two steps up there, a tiny bathroom with a door that wouldn't quite shut. Ralph never criticized anything about Bob's work because he would never risk hurting a relationship. Bob found healing in the Ericksons' home.

During WWII, Ralph joined the Army as a chaplain. Suffering was everywhere. He had volunteered for service and was sent to Europe. Marc was three when his father left. After a tearful goodbye to his dear wife and four young children, he flew out of the airport with the car keys in his pocket, so a locksmith came. There was little time for a mother with four young children to start crying about her husband leaving into the unknowns of WWII. Following the Battle of the Bulge, Ralph got a mastoid ear infection and had to return home. Marc was five years old when his father came back from Europe and he began working in a Veterans Administration Hospital—a psychiatric hospital that gave him a chaplaincy position.

The soldiers came home broken and in pain, what today is referred to as PTSD. The doctors at the hospital didn't have much use for a chaplain, but the nurses liked Ralph, saying he had a better score of seeing men healed than the doctors did. He was a pastor at heart, he enjoyed counseling and praying with troubled, fearful, broken men. He became a student of mental illness, which had a great impact on Marc. Ralph had a special knack of calming patients down. He was their pastor, and he trusted God to heal. People at the hospital were uncomfortable when one particular patient with a paranoid personality disorder would stand behind Ralph when he preached at the chapel services. They were afraid of this patient. But the patient told Ralph he was there to protect him, so no one would hurt him. Ralph told everyone it was fine. Other patients would throw hymn books at him when he preached. They had a lot of anger and fear, but Ralph understood. His voice was booming. He would preach to six people as if he were preaching to a thousand. He sang the same way. He had developed his voice while he was in France and Germany, where the troops would come and sit on logs in an open-air chapel and listen to him.

Near the end of his career, he ministered in a medical VA hospital in Seattle and was on call 24/7. Though they lived twenty miles away from the hospital, he insisted the staff call if anyone asked for him. Ralph didn't want anyone to die alone, so he always got up and went to pray with them at all hours of the night. He spent time getting to know the guys from the VA and often would go bowling with them. Many of the men came to Christ because of him. He didn't just preach the Word, he lived it. When he died, people came from all over because he had led them to Christ. Many were unchurched people, but when they heard the chaplain had died, they all came. They knew he had loved them, and because of that, they came to trust God's love for them.

Ralph knew life was more important than what success from a career or money or recognition could bring. For him, life was all about people, about taking care of relationships, about kindness, and forgiveness. He knew God wanted to love people through him, that's how he lived his life.

CHAPTER 3

Her Roots

*"The God who created names, and numbers the stars
in the heavens also numbers the hairs of my head.
He pays attention to very big things and to very small
ones. What matters to me matters to Him, and that
changes my life."*
— Elizabeth Elliot

Minneapolis, 1949

Meanwhile, Nancy was also being raised in a Christian home. Her parents weren't in ministry like Marc's. Her father, David Brown, was a CPA, and her mother, Florence, worked for him, but they lived their faith strongly and faithfully. Nancy was the second of four children born to her parents. David built a home for the family way out in the country just before Nancy was born. They had no neighbors close by, so family became everything to them. Her parents were Swedish Baptists and helped start a church in the neighborhood. They would always care for neighbors as they moved into the area and would invite them to church. Nancy could see that Jesus was everything to her parents. It was a pretty idyllic childhood, living off the land, enjoying family, and friends.

Family missionaries would come and stay on their property when they were on furlough, so she was introduced to missions from an early age. In those days, you'd be overseas for five years and come home for a year. Her uncle was a surgeon in the Congo and had the most influence on her. He'd bring his slides home of gory surgeries. He'd say, "Do you see this big goiter? Do you see this big tumor? This is how we repaired it!" She would watch it all. They had kids the same ages as she and her siblings, and they had fun. Her parents put a trailer on the back of their property for them. But they always ate meals together.

One of the first places her father worked was at General Mills. There was a big mill along the Mississippi River in Minneapolis, and the offices were filled with flour dust. He'd been a chemistry major and wrote a large report advising a new vacuum air system be put in. He warned the supervisors that the building was unsafe, there could be an explosion, and many would die. They fired David. The building later did blow up, and many people died.

Nancy's parents helped to start a church during the war when all building materials were to go for the war effort, but somebody purchased things on the black market, and they went ahead and began to build. It hurt her father terribly. Integrity was everything to him. It broke his heart and probably instigated their eventual move.

For years, David and Florence looked at houses in Minneapolis. He held on to the hope of moving his family there one day to provide better schools for his children.

Nancy used to hide when her parents went out looking. It was like a spring rite, a parade of homes kind of thing. They'd usually come back and say, "There's no place like home," and she'd be fine again. But one time they came home, and her father said, "I think we found the house. I'm going to take you out of school and show it to you. I want you to know that you'll be happy there!" So he took Nancy to see it.

They pulled up in front of a house in Minneapolis that sat up on a very high hill in a very beautiful neighborhood. It looked like a mansion to her. It was so unlike where they were living, she knew it would be a different world. But already, Nancy reasoned, living in the country, her father had to work such long hours, and her mother would work on Saturdays at the office with him. The responsibility to clean, do laundry and yard and garden work, and care for the younger siblings fell to Nancy and her sister. So when she saw this big house, she said, "Oh, I'm just going to be a full-time maid now," and she started to cry. "Daddy, I don't want to live in this house." She didn't know the reality of many things. He had protected them. All she thought was now he would have to work more hours, and she would only have more responsibility. She didn't want to leave her friends either. It was a hard lump to swallow.

Throughout his married life, Nancy's father had felt a great responsibility for his own mother and six siblings. His own father had died during David's early teen years doing missionary work in Mexico. Now his siblings worked in missions overseas. Everyone depended on David. But that year, his mother had died, and his two sisters who'd lived with her were in a good retirement home. He'd built a cabin for his missionary siblings to stay in when they came home on furlough. So with all this in his mind, he leaned over, put his arm around Nancy, and wiped her tears. "We've had a very heavy load on us helping to support them all," he said. "I'm released from that obligation, and now it's time to buy a home for my family and for my wife, and put my children in good schools."

He did financial planning and taxes for one of the wealthy families in Minneapolis. He could see clearly how to invest for them, but he never had the means to do the same for himself. They'd lived at poverty level. But now, when Nancy was thirteen, they moved into the city of Minneapolis. She began attending a new school but immediately felt like a country bumpkin.

It was a very hard time in her life to make such a big move. She never really felt accepted at her new school. The harder she tried, the more difficult it was. Her mother didn't realize living in town would call for different clothes. To her mother, whatever you wore in the country would be fine in the city. But to a teenager, being in style or out of style mattered. So Nancy found a job at the local library shelving books after school to make money for some new clothes.

She became involved in a program called Young Life, which helped. In the big city school, she knew she wasn't anyone special. She had to wrestle with the Lord to find out who she was and who He was in her life, and how she would know who He wanted her to be. She was developing a deep personal relationship with the Living God. One day, she felt

Him clearly speak to her heart. It was a very special day that changed her entire life. She knew now that she wanted to live for God and decided to let Him lead. That was a pivotal day, and she never turned back after that. That day, she knew in her heart that she didn't have to be accepted by the kids anymore; she didn't have to be a super anything. She belonged to God.

The youth group at their church was strong. She invited them to their house every Sunday night. By that point, she worked in a bakery that only served things that were baked that day. They never kept anything overnight, so they'd send home coffee cakes and cookies, and she'd put it all in the freezer. On Sunday nights, she'd invite her friends over, and there was always plenty to serve. Her mother never had to be nervous about hosting the group. The kids would come and sing and play the piano and hang out for hours. It was a very sweet fellowship. In the summers, they camped together. So she made friends with the youth group at their church and finally felt she belonged.

~

During her college years, Nancy's treasured maternal grandfather had a heart attack. He was not expected to live. She had just begun dating Marc. She longed to visit her Grandpa once more. Marc borrowed a car and took her to the hospital in Chicago. As he stood beside her waiting for the elevator, tears slipped down her cheeks. She could hear her heart pounding as she stood close to him and worried he could hear it too. He pressed the elevator button for the 4th floor, and they rode up in silence. As they walked side by side down the long sterile corridor toward the waiting room for family members only, Marc felt uncomfortable. He had not met her family yet, but he was with her. And that was what mattered.

Grandpa Helge Erickson had come to the U.S. as an immigrant from Sweden when he was eighteen to represent his family at his brother's wedding. But the boat had been late, and he arrived the day after the wedding. He didn't have a return ticket, so he stayed and found work. He eventually became a watchmaker apprentice and later bought the jewelry store where he worked on Clark Street in Chicago. He married his Anna, and they had four daughters. His second daughter, Florence, married a CPA named David Brown, so her family name was Brown, but her grandfather on her mother's side's name was Erickson.

Nancy's Mother and Dad and her mother's three sisters were at the hospital that day with their husbands. She introduced Marc to everyone. After each of his daughters and their husbands had spent time in the ICU with Helge, they looked at Nancy and said she could go in to see him, but just for three minutes.

"Very short," they said. 'Because he is so weak."

Worried she was losing her grandpa with only several minutes of time to be with him, she did her best to hold back her tears.

"How did you get here?" Grandpa asked as she walked into the room.

"My boyfriend, Marc Erickson, brought me, Grandpa."

"Well, I want to know about him," he said with a twinkle in his eyes. So she told him all about him. "I want to meet him! Go get him and bring him in here." So out she went to bring Marc in. Her mother and aunts thought it was ridiculous.

After some conversation between the three of them, Grandpa Helge spoke to Marc. "I had four daughters. The son that I had died as a small child. I have no one to carry on my name. You marry her."

Nancy let out a nervous giggle and could barely look at Marc. "Grandpa!" Until that time, she hadn't even thought about the commonality of their names.

So Marc had trumped everybody because he was an Erickson. Grandpa Helge recovered and lived several more years. He had a happiness gene which was passed on to Nancy. Marc had seen it and fallen in love with her. When Helge told stories, he would start laughing before he could finish. Tears would be rolling down his cheeks as they waited for the punch line. He entertained himself as much as the rest of them.

Helge loved the Lord! When the depression came, he and some Christian friends from their Swedish church bought some land in Michigan where they could bring inner-city youth to camp and tell them of Christ. He was full of joy and loved to sing. Being a jeweler during the depression wasn't easy. He had many difficulties in life and had to move his family time and again when they lost properties, but through it all, Jesus was enough for him. Finally, he was able to purchase his own store on Clark Street in Chicago.

CHAPTER 4

The Engagement

"Believe in a love that is being stored up for you like an inheritance, and have faith that in this love there is a strength and a blessing so large that you can travel as far as you wish without having to step outside it."
— *Rainer Maria Rilke*

Minneapolis, Minnesota 1960

Summer arrived, lilacs perfumed the Midwestern air, and bridal's wreath burst into miniature bouquets, just as they did every year. But now, to Nancy, it was as if all of nature were acknowledging a love that had been divinely orchestrated. The semester came to a close, and she went home to Minneapolis. Marc returned to Seattle and spoke to his mother about the state of his heart. He had fallen in love and wanted to go to visit Nancy and tell her how God was leading him. His mother reminded him he would need a ring. That was not the sort of thing he had thought of, and it presented a dilemma—he didn't have extra cash. How timely. His mother had just happened to walk into a jewelry store filled with balloons for a big promotion. Inside one of them was a prize, a discount on a diamond. "You might like

29

this coupon I won," she grinned. They went back to the store together to pick out an engagement ring for Nancy.

Marc wrote to Nancy asking if he could come to visit, so she wrote a long letter to her parents, who were at her grandparents' cabin in Michigan. She wanted them to come home so Marc could come to get to know them. They had really only said hello and goodbye to Marc before that. She told them what she saw in Marc, that she loved him and how special he was. Her grandpa perceptively said, "He's going to bring a ring. You be there." She had no clue. They came home, and Marc came with a ring. All along, her grandpa felt Marc was a son to him. As soon as Marc knew he was invited, he packed a bag and flew to Minnesota. He couldn't wait any longer.

Marc didn't have a plan for when or how he was going to ask her, or any of the romantic ideas a young man might have at a time such as this. He simply showed up with a ring. The next morning, Nancy was making breakfast in her family's Midwest home. She was surprised when he presented a ring and knelt down before her.

"I love you, Nancy. I want to marry you. Which finger does this go on?"

Chills ran through her as she was simultaneously stunned and overjoyed. Then he told her about the special word he had received. God had spoken to Marc's heart and told him, "I really love this girl, you better promise to take good care of her." Nancy was undone.

"I think you needed to hear that," Marc said. She nodded as she brushed away a tear.

There was only one faux pas. That night at dinner, her parents came home from Michigan and Nancy already had the ring on her finger. Marc had not yet asked her father for his permission. This presented something for David to chew on.

David sat Marc down and asked him if he was prepared to support her and finish paying for her college tuition. He wanted Nancy to finish college. "Of course, it should be that way," Marc agreed. David gave him his blessing and after that everything was fine. He really liked Marc. It was a good way to start. They became fast friends.

Years later, when David had a stroke, Nancy called Marc to let him know that he was dying.

"Who's dying?" Marc asked. He told her to go and check to see if he had an IV running. She dropped the receiver and ran down the hall. He didn't. Marc talked to the doctor.

"David needs fluids," Marc said. "Get an IV in him immediately." They were just waiting for him to die, but Marc wasn't going to stand for that. They gave him an IV and he lived fifteen more years.

CHAPTER 5

Love Meets Faithfulness

"Place me like a seal over your heart,
Like a seal on your arm;
For love is as strong as death,
Its jealousy unyielding as the grave.
It burns like blazing fire,
Like a mighty flame.
Many waters cannot quench love;
Rivers cannot wash it away.
If one were to give all the wealth
of his house for love,
It would be utterly scorned."
(Song of Songs 8:6-7, NIV)

Seattle, Washington 1961

They hoped to be married in a year's time. Marc had
planned to stay in Seattle and attend the University of
Washington, and Nancy planned to return to Wheaton that
year. But as time went on, Marc realized he couldn't be apart
from her for a year. He surprised Nancy and came back to
Wheaton. He could run a fast mile, so he got an athletic
scholarship.

They planned the marriage for the following August. When the time came, Marc and his parents drove from Seattle to Minneapolis for the wedding. He wanted to get there a few days before their wedding, so he planned to drive straight through. Talk about excitement! However, they ended up running out of gas in the middle of North Dakota because of a broken gas gauge. Someone came along and picked them up. They spent the night in a small rural town waiting for parts and repair.

Nancy and her mother made all the wedding plans. Her mother, Florence, had been clear: they would need to limit the number of guests invited to their wedding. Nancy's Aunt Lil was a caterer and had served hundreds of weddings. She wanted the wedding dinner to be her wedding gift to Nancy and Marc. She had planned a lovely supper to be served in the church basement. But she wanted to know the exact number of people coming. Nancy told her probably about 250. However, two weeks before the wedding, there had been an open invitation for a wedding for a new couple in town who didn't know many people in the church. The pastor had made a general announcement from the pulpit to the congregation, saying anyone who wanted to come and witness the wedding was invited. That made people think all weddings were now an open invitation. Everyone in the church knew the Browns. On the wedding day, Aunt Lil and Uncle Marty had been downstairs working all day. They came upstairs when they heard the organ start to play and slipped into the back row and started counting all the people. They quickly realized there were twice as many guests as they had anticipated. They went flying out the back door to buy more groceries. They missed the whole service.

Aunt Lil went to Nancy after the reception all teary-eyed. "Nancy, I always, always pack a special lunch for the bride and groom." She gave Nan a big hug goodbye. "It's my trademark. But today there were no leftovers."

"But you fed all the guests, Aunt Lil!"

As a wedding gift, her parents gave them her mother's nine-year-old car. The next day they packed all of the wedding gifts into the car, ceiling to floor, until there was just barely room for them to sit, and they set off for Seattle. They drove up to Northern Minnesota, crossed into Canada, and then drove west to Seattle. At one point, there was smoke coming out from under the hood of the car.

"Quick, quick!" Marc shouted. "Give me a blanket!"

Nan had to grab one of their new wedding blankets, which he used to put out the fire. They stopped at a gas station in the middle of nowhere to find out what was wrong. It was only a wire from the radio that had burned. There was a woman nine months pregnant and in labor with two little kids hanging on her skirt. She was running the station alone. They wanted to stay and help her, but she didn't want the newlyweds to stay. She just kept saying, "No, no, no. Just go, just go, just go!" So they did and prayed for her for the next 100 miles.

As they neared Calgary, there were signs for peaches everywhere, so they bought a box of peaches. But when they neared the U.S. border, Customs wouldn't allow the fruit across the line. So, instead of crossing, they turned around and went to a picnic table and ate all the peaches they could. They were the best they'd ever eaten, dripping sweet juice down their chins. Still, they couldn't make a dent in them.

Back at the border, they were questioned again, "What is all this stuff in your car?" They were told they would need to take it all out so it could be inspected. Nan thought fast and pulled out their wedding book, where she had recorded all the gifts, and showed it to him. They stamped their wedding book, and they were allowed to drive through.

That night, they were both really sick from all the peaches they'd eaten.

Arriving in Seattle, they moved into their new apartment and found a telegram waiting. Nancy's twelve-year-old brother, Dave, had been in a bike accident and was in a coma. The telegram was already a week old. They didn't know if he was alive or dead; her heart wanted to turn around and go back. She called home for details. Her family lived on a very steep hill, and Dave had been riding down the hill when the bolt from his front tire broke. His wheel flew off, and he went over the handlebars, hitting his head on the pavement. Florence was coming home from the store and saw all the fire trucks.

"Oh no, I won't go that way." She went around the block instead, only to find the firemen standing in her driveway. They told her they had taken Dave to the hospital. Nancy had to pray and learn a new level of trusting God. She couldn't go back. It was a hard lesson at the very beginning of their marriage. She had left family to cleave to her husband. The

35

bike accident had left Dave deaf, shattering the bones in his middle ear. A year and a half later, they did a new surgery, putting artificial bones in, which restored a lot of his hearing.

They had transferred from Wheaton to the University of Washington, Seattle. It was a lot cheaper. Marc had a job there and hoped to go to medical school there. Their apartment was nice, close to a mall, but $150 a month was a little over their budget. Nancy had unwrapped all their gifts, written all the thank-you notes, and gotten settled in. They were both in school, and Marc was never home. On top of his school schedule, he had a job as a night stocker at Safeway and was working forty hours a week. She wanted him to cut back on his hours, but in order to do that, of course, they would need to cut their already tight budget. He had one more year of college, and she had two.

She watched the Want Ads and found an ad for a little cottage that rented for just $45 a month. It was a little garage that had been converted into a guest house. She went and took a look and thought it would make the cutest little love nest. After two months in their first apartment together, they moved. She got a job in a bakery, and they had their nights together. They also worked together at a small church as youth pastors. Nancy taught the junior high kids, and Marc worked with the senior highs. While they had been at Wheaton, a friend of Marc's from a very wealthy family in Seattle was killed in a car accident. Marc had led this friend to Christ. His sister was now in Nancy's junior high youth group.

One Sunday night when the youth group was meeting in the garage, the girl's father came to the door. No one ever came to their tiny house. He had come to ask for a pledge for the church. The church was paying them $10 a month, which they used for gas money for the youth groups. The man saw how they lived compared to how he lived, and he backed out of the door, apologizing. That little visit softened his heart.

Nancy's parents came for a visit on their second anniversary. By this time, Nancy had graduated from the University and was eight months pregnant. Florence was taken aback when she saw how they lived, but David was proud of them. Marc and Nancy had saved $1500. They were happy, they were fed, she had finished school, and her dad wanted to help them find a place where there would be room for a baby. They had been very happy in their little love nest for two years, but she thought her parents were right. They would need more space for a baby, so she found a real estate agent who made it clear that, on their budget, the houses they could afford would either have an outhouse in the back or be far into the countryside. She told Nancy to go look for herself. It wasn't worth her own gas to go. But not long after that, the realtor called back and suggested she might have something. There was a house near the University that came furnished. They could buy it on a land contract. They offered $1500 down plus $85/mo. It was a cute bungalow that had everything they needed. They moved in.

"This is God's abundant blessing!" Nancy was overjoyed.

"And it even came with two toothbrushes!" Marc joked.

A friend from the bakery hired them to paint the outside of her two-story house. They worked from sun up till sun down all week. Nancy handled the trim. She'd climb the extension ladder and paint until she got dizzy, then she'd scramble down, lie on the grass until it passed, and climb back up the ladder. She was nine months pregnant. During that week, she and Marc went to her doctor's appointment. The doctor thought she was overdue and decided to take an x-ray. He walked into the waiting room where they were sitting and showed them the x-ray. He pointed at the x-ray, explaining, "Here's one spine, here's one spine, and here's one spine." Nancy panicked. Then he explained further, one of the spines was hers. Marc was speechless. They were having twins! The first person they told was Grandpa Helge because he was a twin himself. He was thrilled! They would manage two babies just fine. They would trust God.

They finished painting the house, and she went into labor an hour later. Marc was doing his Obstetrics rotation as a sophomore in medical school. His classmates were told about the multiple birth. When Nancy delivered that night at the University hospital, she was a teaching case for fifteen students. The only one who couldn't be there was Marc. They said it was too risky to let the father into the delivery room. She pulled the sheet up over her head. They had two healthy, beautiful baby boys. How times have changed.

Florence flew out to Seattle to meet her first grandchildren, when they were just one week old. While reading the paper, she saw an ad for crates of peaches at Abramson's, a local grocery.

"You should go get them. We can make jam!" her mother

offered. The boys were asleep, so Florence stayed with them while Nancy went. She bought two crates of peaches, and then the key broke off in the car door. She left the crates of peaches sitting outside the car, went into the store, and asked where a locksmith was.

"Six blocks," she was told. So just one week after delivering twins, she walked. She had had many stitches and was very sore, but she walked the six blocks only to find out the locksmith was closed. She asked someone else for help, and they pointed her in the direction of a hardware store. She walked further. It was far. When she finally got home, her mother was beside herself.

"Where have you been?! You've been gone for two hours!" Both boys were hungry and crying. She wasn't too happy with Nancy, but she couldn't blame her.

They had a college ministry at that time and were planning a Christmas party for the students. Nancy was baking cookies for them, and the boys were in two bassinets in the kitchen. She'd use her foot to rock one while she fed the other. They were close enough to the neighbor's house that she noticed a woman in her window next door waving at her. The woman finally came over.

"This is a three-ring circus. How can I help?" she cried. God sends angels!

Three months later, Nancy started teaching school, and Marc's mom watched the boys for her. Delnora was her most treasured friend. Ministries don't happen in a vacuum. Without their parents, they would not have survived.

CHAPTER 6

Determination

*"Never be lacking in zeal, but keep your spiritual
fervor, serving the Lord."*
(Romans 12:1, NIV)

Seattle to St. Paul

The University Presbyterian Church was a big, influential church in downtown Seattle. The pastor, Bob Munger, was a leader in world missions, and Marc had heard him speak during the time he was at Wheaton and wanted to pick his brain. He really didn't know what he was doing when he walked up to Dr. Munger's office and asked the secretary if he could talk to the pastor about missions.

"Do you have an appointment?"

"No."

"You don't have an appointment?" She asked again.

"No." Marc shook his head but didn't back away.

The secretary stared at him. Marc waited. "Just a minute," she finally relented. "I'll go ask him."

Within minutes, Dr. Munger came out of his office, and Marc followed him in. He thought God must have spoken to Dr. Munger because for the next several hours, he told Marc everything he knew about missions in the Middle East. He was on the board for Presbyterian Missions and had worked in rural India and the Middle East. He knew everything Marc needed to learn in order to prepare for his calling into missions. Marc was twenty years old, and he'd just been briefed on the spiritual situation in the Middle East by Dr. Munger. He had opened the door for Marc, and Marc instinctively knew God was leading him. He didn't have any idea at the time, but that visit with Dr. Munger continued to have a powerful influence on his life over the next forty years.

~

Nancy graduated in Elementary Education and taught for three years until Marc graduated from medical school. There was then a move to St. Paul for Marc to do a 'rotating internship', which was how you became a general practitioner in those days. Again, she rarely saw him. They lived in city housing, which was newly built but very flimsy with poor heat. Minnesota winters were cold. Their car froze up every time it got cold. They did their best to keep their little car going that winter.

Nancy was now pregnant for the second time. As the due date approached, Marc was worried that she wouldn't get to the hospital in time. One night, he came home believing he had received a nudge from God.

"OK, I'm starting OB rotation and I'm on call tomorrow. I won't be home again for several days, so let's have this baby tonight."

"What? Are you going to induce labor?"

"No, you're going to go into labor."

"Honey, I'm so tired, just let me go to bed."

"No," Marc said. "You're going to stay up and go into labor." So he tried to teach her how to play chess, but she couldn't concentrate. At midnight, they asked the neighbor lady to watch the twins and went to the hospital. Sure enough, by the time they got there, Nancy was having contractions.

When the two of them walked into the hospital, one of the staff said, "Marc, you're not on call tonight."

"I know. My wife is in labor." OB was very busy; they had some complicated deliveries at the moment. One woman's baby was transverse, and they couldn't turn the baby. She needed a C-section, so they put Marc to work right away. Nancy was progressing; the intensity of her contractions was increasing. She began to wonder if someone would be in to check on her. She waited all night.

Finally, someone did come. "I'm ready to deliver," Nancy said. They checked. She was. They rushed her into a delivery room, and it was Marc who delivered Paul, while her doctor stood watching. He had assumed Marc was the OB resident. Nancy had had complications with bleeding all throughout the pregnancy, and the placenta had deteriorated. Paul was born purple and not breathing. Marc breathed for him for the first ten minutes of his life before they brought in oxygen. Still, the baby was struggling, and Nancy was informed that he probably wouldn't make it.

The doctor washed up, took off his skull cap, and went to stand beside Marc. "Oh!" the doctor was taken aback. "I didn't realize you were the baby's father!"

So they went from the first delivery where Marc couldn't be there to the second where he delivered the baby. Thank God because he breathed life into their baby, and Paul survived.

After a day-and-a-half of Marc being on the floor and not being able to stop in to see Nancy, she became very depressed. She hadn't seen the baby yet; she started crying and couldn't stop.

"I'm going home," she told the doctor. And she did. She took her baby and went to see her mother. Florence helped her, and Paul started eating and did great. He was their gift from St. Paul. He was named for two special Pauls. The first was her Uncle Paul, who had influenced her with his work in missions and poured life into her. The second was Paul Burkhardt, Marc's running buddy at Wheaton, a competitive rascal. But Marc had slowly influenced him to come to know Christ, and he became a different man, eventually going into mission work in Indonesia with an unreached tribal group.

After Paul's birth, once again, they started a little home Bible Study in their apartment in St. Paul with a half dozen people. There was an unmarried pregnant woman, and another man in the study who had his eye on her.

When it came time to deliver, Nancy and this friend had their babies at about the same time. The woman had a complete breakdown after delivery. She had to be put in a psychiatric ward, and the baby was put in foster care.

This dear mother escaped from the hospital one day that winter to find her baby. Apparently, while she and some patients were in the gym, she saw her chance to run and took it. The hospital called Nancy to see if she had come to their house. Nancy left her own kids with the neighbor and drove around looking for her. She found the woman walking barefoot in her gym shorts and top in the freezing cold! She told her to get in the car and wrapped her in the blankets she had brought along. The woman begged her not to take her back to the hospital. Nancy told her she'd have to go back, but brought her home to their house first. When they arrived, the woman picked up Paul and shouted, "This is my baby, this is my baby."

"No, that's my baby," Nancy tried to stay calm. Then the woman grabbed a knife, and with Paul in one hand and the knife in the other, started to run.

"It's my baby!" The woman screamed. Nancy chased her down two flights of construction steps, tackled her, and rescued Paul. Then Nancy found a neighbor and thrust Paul into her arms, explaining that she had to take her friend back to the hospital. She called ahead, and they sent someone down to meet them. It was so hard to take her back. She really had given her life to Christ, but for some reason, went through that dark, dark period. The man from the Bible Study eventually married her, and the baby was returned. God's grace was greater than they could have ever imagined.

There were times being without Marc that year that were hard, but they thought when he finally finished his internship, they would be released to begin their lives as missionaries. They applied to a well-respected mission board. The application was arduous. First, they had to take extensive Bible and theology tests to prove their preparation and qualifications for the job. Nancy worried Marc would pass, but she would not. But she did pass. God's grace is abundant.

Then they were invited to come to New York to meet with the mission leadership. To fly to New York City for them was a big deal. Neither had ever been to New York, and they had no money. They stayed at the mission headquarters and were given the address of the psychiatrist they were supposed to see and the time of their appointment. The psychiatrist was to verify their adaptability and emotional stability to be sent overseas. Not knowing NYC, they mapped out the route, walked across Central Park to get there, and returned after dark. The mission staff was furious with them.

"You never do that!" they were told. "Take a taxi!"

Marc and Nancy hadn't known the potential danger or even had the money to take the taxi. But God had used that experience, too, to remove their fear. They were so excited. They had thought their dreams were finally going to happen.

While still in med school in Seattle, they had met a doctor named Linn McClenny, a missionary from Sudan. He had been forced out of Sudan and had gone to Ethiopia. When they heard his story, God grabbed hold of their imagination. This is the place and person Marc thought he'd like to work with. They began to pray and look forward to going to Ethiopia to work with Dr. McClenny in a place called Shashamane. That plan continued to grow in them through med school and internship. Then all of a sudden in 1967, Marc got a draft notice from the Army. For five years, he had been deferred from the draft while he was finishing medical school and internship training. They had thought the Vietnam War would be over by then. They notified the mission board of their draft notice. The board told them they could file an exemption for humanitarian service, but Marc and Nancy weren't satisfied with that answer, trusting God knew the timing. They reasoned that God might send them overseas at the Army's expense, giving them language and the broader cultural experiences they longed for.

Marc was asked to send a list to the Army of his ten top choices for service. Together, Marc and Nancy listed everything from Ethiopia to Saudi Arabia to Vietnam. Marc reasoned that God might send him to Vietnam to teach him tropical medicine. Then they waited again. Finally, he got his orders. It was to Milwaukee, Wisconsin. They thought, "What? Who wants to go there!" All they knew about Milwaukee was beer, and they weren't drinkers. But orders were orders. Before moving to Milwaukee, Marc was sent to San Antonio, Texas for Army training, while Nan was to move the family to Milwaukee. Her friend Joy from their Bible study volunteered to go to Milwaukee with her to find a place for them to live.

CHAPTER 7

Change in Plans

"God doesn't need us, what He does, though, is open up
a space for us to be needed."
— Marc Erickson

Milwaukee, Wisconsin 1968

It was a very dark time. Dr. Martin Luther King Jr. had just been assassinated. Milwaukee was under martial law; many streets were barricaded. Nancy drove with Joy through the city, passing boarded-up buildings, smashed storefronts, through littered streets, many with yellow tape at intersections causing them to drive round and round, getting lost in detours. There was block after block of destruction and devastation caused by the riots, anger and grief and injustice of the Black community.

Through all the sadness, they came upon the most beautiful vista—Lake Michigan! Beyond the sandy beach, was sparkling water that reached beyond the horizon. They parked and praised God right there on the beach, believing He had a place for them.

They bought a newspaper and began searching the Want Ads for the cheapest, the very cheapest, places. And they looked and looked. The boys had told her to find a house where they could have a puppy, so that was in the back of her mind. They saw apartments and townhouses, and finally found a townhouse that seemed suitable. They gave the landlord a down payment. Then they drove back to Minneapolis to collect the boys.

Nancy's parents told her they would give them a washer and dryer if she could figure out what kind of hook-ups there were in the townhouse.

Organized and efficient, she called the landlord to find out if the dryer hook-up was gas or electric. All she was able to reach was a recording that the phone had been disconnected. "I called the Better Business Bureau only to find out that the man who rented the townhouse to me was wanted all over the city for taking people's money." She had stepped right into a scam. He didn't own the property. So she quickly called the bank, and fortunately they were able to stop payment on the check. But now there was no place to move to and the movers were already scheduled. She kept pushing forward and called the doctor that Marc would be replacing at the Armed Forces Examining Station (AFES), asking if he could go check out one other possibility. He agreed and called her back.

"He asked if I was a hard worker." She assured him she was, so he thought it might be a home for a family. It was definitely a fixer-upper. With that, she called this landlord and sent him two months' rent as a deposit. She rented the house, sight unseen. Her sister, Bev, drove with her and the boys back to Milwaukee. When they arrived that night, there were no locks on the doors and not a lightbulb in the place.

It was the scariest dark place, and Bev was adamant that she would not stay there.

In the back of her wallet was a credit card Nancy had received when she got her teaching certificate. It had never been used, but she thought maybe it would work. They found a Holiday Inn and stayed there overnight. The next morning, they went back to see the house by daylight. It was worse than either of them could have ever dreamed. They stepped inside and the stench of urine was nauseating. Bev refused to take another step and took the boys to a school playground up the street. Nancy knew the work needed on the house was way beyond her ability to fix, but what could she do?

While Bev was at the playground with the boys, she found a Sears store and opened a credit card, bought some paint and cleaning supplies. Then she returned to the house and started scrubbing.

"One room," I told myself. "I can clean one room." So she scrubbed down the living room and was just finishing it when the moving truck drove up with their furniture. She watched as a couple of college-aged guys walked up to the door.

They took one look inside and stopped.

"Just give me a little bit of time," she said. "If I can paint this one room, you can unload everything into it." The two young men each picked up a brush and helped her paint until four o'clock that afternoon. One room was clean. They unloaded the truck into that room. When Bev returned with the boys, she spent the night, but had to leave first thing in the morning. Nancy started working her way through the house—cleaning floors with holes, pulling out liquor bottles that were stashed everywhere. The plumbing didn't work, the toilet sat on a floor that was rotten. She bought a Styrofoam cooler to keep milk in, put the babies in a playpen, unpacked her electric fry pan and put it on the floor to sterilize bottles and cook their meals.

Across the street lived two little old sisters, probably in their nineties, who were watching all this. One day, they came over to visit. They said they saw her painting, sometimes at three or four in the morning, and inquired if she ever slept. Nancy assured them that she did, but since she had to be with the children during the day, she got as much done during the night as she could. They were very sweet to her and the boys and returned with a little plastic bag. "Put the laundry for the children in here, and we will do it for you." She thought to herself about the mountain of laundry the children produced and wondered what to put in the little bag. But she filled it up, and they washed those clothes, bringing back the little tops and diapers and pants all neatly folded—with cookies on top. They would do that every three or four days, and Nan would stop work and talk to them and love on them.

By Thanksgiving, she had finally finished cleaning, painting, and repairing the house as much as possible. Marc came home, and they were a family again. The house looked good too. Marc never understood all she had done. When the landlord came, he wanted to up the rent because of all the improvements she had made. "Over my dead body!" she roared. "I'm the one who made this house livable!"

50

There was nothing but a porcelain sink falling off the wall in the kitchen. It was slanted so that if she washed dishes and set them on the drain board, they would slide right onto the floor. There were no counters or cupboards. The landlord finally came and put some cupboards in and redid the holey kitchen and bathroom floors.

They later learned the house had been part of an inheritance and was a tax write-off. The previous owners were alcoholics and didn't care about it. The new owner had never seen it. But it really turned into a blessing. The boys got their puppy! Nan bought pieces of fence from the Want Ads for $20 and dug some post holes in the backyard. She built a fence for the boys and the puppy.

Marc came home one day from his army job at the examining station and found the boys pounding boards together on the driveway. He asked them what they were doing. They explained they were building a treehouse. Marc said, "Why don't we start with a tree?" So they moved the boards to a tree in the yard, and that became a great father-son project. They had a lot of fun in that treehouse.

~

During the two years they were living in Milwaukee, Marc worked giving induction physicals to draftees. He only bought one uniform. Every night, Nancy washed it, and every day, he wore it. He was clear: he was not going to waste money on a second uniform. Marc worked moonlighting at different hospitals several nights a week so they could earn their passage overseas and whatever they would need to take with them. They never lost sight of their goal. Marc was working long, hard hours while Milwaukee was still under martial law. Every draftee in Wisconsin came through that station. The rural farm guys in Wisconsin were patriots, willing to give their lives for their country. The University guys were all protesting the war and would not go. Some lied about ailments, and some covered up their ailments. He hated that the physicals had to be done in groups of twenty at a time. It was dehumanizing, like a cattle call. Marc had to figure out what the truth was for every young man he saw.

CHAPTER 8

Pride's Gotta Go

"Circumcision is circumcision of the heart, by the Spirit not by the written code. Such a man's praise is not from men, but from God."
(Romans 2:29, NIV)

Milwaukee, Wisconsin, 1968

A new home meant a new Bible study. They had a few couples join. One man who came would promptly fall asleep, and his wife, on the other hand, would not stop talking.

One day, Marc was up in the attic having his devotions and came down the staircase crying. He sat on the steps, tears streaming, "Nan, God just spoke to me. I'm not ready to serve the Lord. I was reading in Romans 2, there has to be a circumcision of the heart. It's not physical. Your pride has to be cut out." He told her he just realized he'd been doing everything all wrong. He thought he could give himself to God, that he had talents and abilities God could use. "But I don't," he said. "God doesn't need me. I quit."

Nancy sat down beside him and cried too. She said, "I believe God can still use us." They prayed together and asked God to circumcise their hearts and remove the pride. That was the beginning of a new life for the couple. They stopped trying to do God's work—and asked God to take over and use them wherever He could.

Within two days, one of Marc's partners confided in him that he was an alcoholic. He asked Marc to tell him how he could know Christ, so Marc shared the Gospel with him, and the man gave his life to Christ that day. After that, people started coming to their Bible studies. During those two years in Milwaukee, they had the house so full of people, they would have to open all the windows across the living room and put chairs and benches on the front porch for overflow. All the while they were saying, "We can't do this ourselves, please use us, Christ." And that became the theme of their life. "If God is in you, let Him do it."

They attended a Baptist Church on the North Side of Milwaukee and were asked if they would teach the college students. It was announced in church that there would be a college meeting at the Ericksons' house that night. Marc and Nancy had a little laugh on the way home from church because they'd never seen a college student at the church. But Marc attended the evening service that night while Nan stayed home to put the kids to bed. She baked cookies and then laid down. All of a sudden, she heard the front door pushed open and male voices inside the house. A group of young men entered the house shouting.

"Is anybody here? Anybody here? We heard there's a Bible study here!"

Nancy came to acknowledge the young men, smelling of

marijuana, wearing neither shirts nor shoes, then went back to tuck the babies in and pray. Before long, Marc arrived and ended up sitting down on the floor with this group of young men, some from the church, and some working for Father Groppi's commandos. Father Groppi was a well-known Catholic priest in Milwaukee who mobilized youth to lead peaceful marches for civil rights and fair-housing laws without racial discrimination, particularly in 1967-1968, and in the aftermath of Dr. King's assassination in April 1968. Nancy wasn't at all intimidated by the rather boisterous young men. Dr. Munger, who had been so instrumental in preparing Marc for work in the mission field, was fighting for anti-discrimination in housing all throughout the time they lived in Seattle. Marc said he could relate to why they weren't going to church anymore. He shared what it now meant to him to be a Christian. When he stopped trying to be a Christian, in his own strength and let Christ live His Life in and through him, everything began to change. He wanted them to discover and know the indwelling Christ. It had been such a big thing for him to experience that Christ brought the power, that He is the engine in one's Christian life. It was important they learn to depend on Him for themselves and then experience His power. Because then, things would start to get exciting.

Many of the young men returned the following week and began to regularly attend the study. Marc and Nancy began to see lives transformed by Jesus, and that was thrilling!

CHAPTER 9

Slow Down, Hurry Up

"Do not drag behind or run ahead; do no shout or keep silent, but devoutly, with great sweetness, with natural simplicity, without any affectation, offer your praise to God with the whole of your heart and soul."
— *Mother Teresa*

Milwaukee, Wisconsin, 1969

Near the end of their time in Milwaukee, their first daughter Lisa was born. During that Christmas holiday, Marc went to a Medical Assistance Program (MAP) seminar in Wheaton, Illinois. There he saw a picture of a 12th-century mosque overlooking the Indian Ocean as he was coming down a stairway and felt God speak to him. The picture was from Somalia.

"Nan, I think we're going to go to Somalia," he said when he returned home.

"Where is Somalia?" she asked.

"Get a map," he said. Somalia wasn't in the news at the time. They had been planning and praying for Ethiopia for so long. Now, they started learning everything they could about its neighbor, Somalia. Their army commitment was almost over. The hippie students that came for Bible study each week wanted to help them get overseas. One day, they passed around a yellow legal pad asking anyone that wanted to, to sign up to help support the Ericksons' mission work in Africa. Enough people signed up for $10 a month that they had their entire support. They had been told they would need to raise $3600 a year for their family's needs.

Marc called mission headquarters to let them know that he would be discharged on Memorial Day weekend. After that, they would be ready to go. Nancy's and Marc's sisters came to help them get ready for Africa. Nan needed their help because she was trying to get rid of everything she could while at the same time trying to figure out what essentials they would need for the five years ahead of them. In those days, you were sent out for five-year terms and then had a one-year furlough. She shopped for shoes to cover five years of growth for the four children. She didn't know what all they would need, so she wrote to the mission office to find out. But what the mission office had to say in return was that they needed to do deputation, they needed to raise support first. Marc told them they didn't have to because the students from their Bible Study had covered it. They had already given everything away, they were mostly packed and ready to go. They had already told the landlord that they were moving out on Memorial Day, sold their car, and given their furniture away to a doctor couple coming back from Ethiopia. They had nothing but their suitcases left and had already shipped fourteen barrels of belongings to New York. The mission was stunned and unprepared.

"Wait, wait!" the mission's administrator said. "We don't have your visas ready for you yet, or your tickets!"

"We thought of those things," Nancy told him. "We earned the money for our tickets, but we were told the mission was supposed to take care of our visas. She did her best not to become exasperated as she waited for their response.

The mission decided to send them to Los Angeles for mission training school first. That would take up time for them to get their visas.

"How are we going to do that?" Nancy asked. "We have nothing left. We're ready to get on an airplane!"

Her father helped them buy a used car, and they put the kids in the station wagon and drove to Los Angeles for six weeks of missionary training. They stayed in the dorms at Biola University during the summer and got to meet many great people. During the training, they were told to go into the city and go door to door sharing the Four Spiritual Laws, an evangelistic tract of Campus Crusade. That type of cold calling was difficult, but they learned and experienced God working.

After they completed the six weeks of training, there was still no news of visas. They drove up to Seattle to say goodbye to Marc's family. It was his parents' 40th anniversary. They were thankful to be there, but the whole time, they kept calling the mission for next steps.

"Do you have our visas? Do you have our passports? Do you have our tickets? Do you have everything?" But no decision had been made even about where to send them. The mission said they couldn't go to Somalia, but perhaps they could go to Ethiopia. But the next day, they suggested sending Marc to Nigeria, but Nigeria was currently having a civil war. The family would have to stay in the States, but they could use Marc.

"No, we are a team," Marc said. "I can't accept that." In addition, Marc was confident that he had received a message from the Lord; they would be going to Somalia. He wasn't going to let anyone change that.

So they loaded the kids and all the luggage into the car, drove from Seattle to Minneapolis to say goodbye to Nancy's family. Then they drove on to Washington DC to see Nan's older sister and husband. They welcomed the family of six despite having no idea how long it would take the mission to move them on. Nancy kept wondering how this could happen? They had burned all bridges and only had what could fit in the car. They prayed! They called and kept calling the mission office.

"Have you got a plan for us yet?" They kept asking again and again.

Finally, Marc and Nancy were told to come to New York. The plan was to send them to work temporarily in Ethiopia while they waited for an opening to Somalia.

Nancy's brother-in-law, Harold, drove them to New York and said one last goodbye. They spent the night in bunkbeds at headquarters on 47th Street. In the morning, missions told them, "Good luck, God bless you," and there was a taxi waiting. It was the day of the twins' sixth birthday—their gift was the trip. Paul was two-and-a-half and Lisa was ten months. Once again, they loaded everyone and everything into a taxi and headed to Kennedy Airport.

Every item going with them had been weighed and measured. Nancy was told seventy pounds per person. Since the mission hadn't answered any of her questions, she had packed one dish per person, one glass, one set of silverware, one pan to cook in, one bed sheet per person, and clothes. She didn't know what would be available in Somalia, and now they were being sent to Ethiopia.

At check-in, she realized no one had told them they had no baggage allowance for the baby. Now they would either have to pay for seventy extra pounds or dispose of seventy pounds. Marc started telling her to get rid of this and get rid of that.

"I can't!" She groaned. "We're down to so little! I can't go around the world with four babies and nothing!" But they couldn't afford the overage, so she started going through everything and then noticed that Marc had at least seventy pounds of medical books in the bags. "Unload some of your books!"

"I cannot go to "Timbuktu" and try to practice medicine without any books!" There would be no library. This was before the Internet. By that point, Nan thought they might have a divorce. That was the biggest conflict they had ever had.

"Dispose of those sweaters," he said.

She had knit a sweater for each of the children, thinking one sweater would suffice in case it got cold. She had knit them with her own hands.

"They weigh next to nothing! And you think I should throw them away?" She began to cry. Walking around the airport to try to work through her emotions while they were waiting for the flight, she spotted a tour group lined up at the counter. They all had yellow vinyl tour bags. She went up to the head of the group.

"Do you happen to have six extra bags I could have?"

"I do." She looked Nancy over, clearly seeing her distress. "What do you need them for?"

"I really need them," was all she could manage to say. The woman gave her six bags. Nancy took them and went running back to Marc and the kids and stuffed all the medical books inside. The only thing she hadn't figured out was that the kids couldn't lift them. Their flight was called for boarding. There they were, Marc had Lisa on his back in a Gerry pack, Nancy took the boys by their hands, they had their carry-ons, and the extra bags of books.

"Hurry up, hurry up! We're going to be late for the flight!" Marc kept hollering.

Then all of a sudden, out of nowhere, the whole flight crew came by, and each one picked up a child and a yellow vinyl bag of books.

"Thank you, God," Nancy kept saying as the crew put them on the airplane.

Neither of them had been out of the country before and they hadn't realized there was a layover in Frankfurt. Missions had given them $60 to use if they needed something, but that was all the cash they had. They had no credit cards or travelers' checks. In Frankfurt, the taxi drivers kept coming up to them saying, "Taxi! Come on! Get in!" Marc insisted, no taxi." They sat down and looked at their tickets and found out it was a twenty-hour layover in Frankfurt. One taxi driver would not leave them alone. As they moved on, he kept pushing and, finally, there they were in his taxi.

"I don't know what we're doing, we can't speak German and we have no money," Marc said. They didn't understand what the driver was saying, and he drove them a long way out of town to the edge of the Black Forest where they came upon a beautiful hotel and stopped.

"Just stay here," Marc said. "I've got to find someone who speaks English." He went inside while the taxi driver was putting all their things in the hotel, and Nancy was wondering what was going on. Finally, they were taken to a room. Everything was beautiful; it was perfectly kept and sanitized. There was even paper over the sanitized toilet. Marc said not to touch a thing, then went to the lobby to look for assistance. He knew he couldn't pay for this hotel. By the time he returned to say he couldn't find anyone who spoke English, they had all laid down on the beds on top of the bedspreads and closed their eyes. That's how they spent the night.

The next morning, they went down to the lobby and let the staff know that they hadn't touched anything. But the desk person told them it had all been covered. The hotel and breakfast were part of their ticket! So they ate breakfast, got back in the taxi, and flew on to Addis Ababa, the capital of Ethiopia.

PART TWO

Whose Are You?

CHAPTER 10

A New Landscape

"The real voyage of discovery consists not in seeing new landscapes but in having new eyes."
— *Marcel Proust*

Addis Ababa, Ethiopia, October 1969

In the wide street and heavy traffic, a donkey traveled with a bundle twice its size strapped horizontally to its back. A woman in a light-colored dress and shawl with her head wrapped in a turban walked alongside barefoot. Tall buildings silhouetted the surrounding mountains. Goods and wares hung from crowded open-aired market stalls, and lepers begged in the streets as uniformed children crisscrossed the pavement of a schoolyard. They arrived at the Sudan Interior Mission (SIM) headquarters, which was like a dormitory for families coming and going. They dropped off their bags and set out for a walk with Marc carrying Lisa in the Gerry pack. Men didn't ordinarily do that in Africa, and soon they looked like Pied Pipers. First, one child was following them, then another, and soon another. Every time Nancy turned around, there were more children, until hundreds had gathered, trying to touch the white people. She began to wonder if she should be afraid.

Finally, they were in Ethiopia. They didn't know the language, they didn't know where they were going, they were just trying to get outside and breathe some air. They knew that many African cities were filled with huge sections so poverty-stricken that people were afraid to go there, but in Addis, the whole city was like this, so poor, with lepers everywhere. Nan may have had some second thoughts about bringing their children to this unknown place, unsure of what they were heading into with so little money, but if so, she kept it to herself. Marc may have been wondering the same thing but remained silent as they walked together through the activity of this fascinating place. They both knew God knew why they were there, and that was sufficient.

After a night's rest at headquarters, the family and their supplies were loaded into a van, then taken down-country seven hours. The road to the mission's compound in Shashamane was precarious with its overhanging cliffs. For the next six weeks, Marc was scheduled to train at the SIM Hospital with Dr. McClenny, the greatest, most compassionate, ingenious doctor he had ever met. He would teach him what was needed to serve as a medical missionary in Somalia.

~

Shashamane's lush jungle was in a mountainous region of East Africa with beautiful lakes. The Little Dadaba River, the color of the golden dirt roads, ran along the edge of the town. Women sat crouched alongside the river, scooping water with gourds. A skinny man in a hat with agile, dusty legs filled a jug as a woman braided hemp nearby. A toothy young girl looked up and smiled amidst the brilliantly colored tropical flowers.

If they had followed the river all the way down, they would eventually end up in Bulo Burte, Somalia, the very spot they were headed. They felt affirmed that God knew what He was doing. Shashamane had farms in place that fed everyone. The village was very well thought out. The mission station was similar to a huge farm that grew corn. Situated at eight thousand feet, there was frost in the water barrel in the mornings, and by afternoon, it reached the mid-70s.

The house they would be staying in was made of timbers set up on bricks with one bedroom that had space for a double bed, a couple of twin beds, and a crib. There was a wood cook stove, the floors were rough wood, and there was an outhouse behind. There were also a lot of bugs and rats. They were told to be careful, not to ever give the baby a bottle in her crib for fear that rats would come and eat the nipple off the bottle. The rats were aggressive, they said, and would eat the feet right out of the baby's pajamas. Nancy had always been terrified of mice, so she asked for help from the mission station and was given a huge steel rat trap.

There was a lean-to off their bedroom with a shower that had a slatted floor to drain the water. She placed the trap inside the shower, locked the door, and shoved some towels underneath. In the night, she shuddered as she heard sounds: Slap! Thump! Thump, thump, thump. The next morning, she told Marc to check the trap, but it was gone. When she went back to the mission station to give her report, they told her she was very green. The trap needed to be nailed down.

After they caught several rats, all she could think was, "Lord, if I see another rat, I'm going home!" But then she told herself she just wouldn't look. That was her introduction to Africa.

It was a challenge to keep the kids fed cooking on the wood stove, but she learned quickly and baked bread daily. They tried to make fun out of everything. A man named Solomon needed work to feed his family, so Nancy hired him to come for a few hours each morning. The first morning, he looked at her floor, ran his hands across it, then looked at her and shook his head. The following morning, he came with kerosene and rags. He treated the floor and then tied the rags on his bare feet and began skating across the floor to polish it. The boys watched and thought it was the best thing in the world; they tied rags on their feet and skated right along with Solomon until the floor was made smooth.

A brilliant surgeon from Australia, Dr. Barry Hicks, and his wife Robin were one of the couples serving at the SIM hospital. Dr. Hicks had arrived by way of Vellore, India, where he had worked with Dr. Paul Brand, a world-famous pioneer in leprosy treatment. Dr. Brand had discovered answers to leprosy and reconstructive hand surgery for the patients. Nobody had really understood leprosy up until that point. Doctors were too busy trying to save thousands of people who were losing their noses, fingers, and ears. Dr. Brand figured out that it wasn't the leprosy itself destroying their bodies, but the rats in the leper colonies that would come and nibble them off in the night. Leprosy took away any sense of pain, so patients were unable to feel the sensation. Once Dr. Brand understood this, they built a hospital and filled it with cats to eat the rats.

While he trained in Vellore, Dr. Hicks sent his wife, Robin, also a trained doctor, and their boys, David and Andrew, ahead of him to Shashamane. But while he was in India, he contracted hepatitis and lost forty pounds. Nobody was sure whether he would survive. When Robin finally picked him up at the airport in Addis, he was skin and bones. The mission put him in their rest house to gain some weight and strength before beginning any work in the hospital. But Barry didn't want to just rest. So he taught himself Amharic, the national language of Ethiopia, and learned other languages as well while he was supposed to be resting and recuperating.

David and Andrew were a year older and a year younger than the Erickson twins, Marc and Mike. Since both Hicks parents were working in the hospital, they asked if Nancy would take care of their boys and homeschool them. So while they were in Shashamane, Nancy began teaching the four boys to read. They were eager students and pushed each other every day.

One Sunday, the staff offered to lend Marc and Nancy a car so they could take the children somewhere special. They hadn't yet seen anything off the compound since their arrival. They were told about a lake nearby, so Nan packed a picnic lunch, and the family set off for a new adventure. On the way, they found a beautiful spot, a little knoll with trees arching over that looked like the perfect location for their lunch. They laid out the blanket and all sat down and prayed. One after another, the children's chins lifted up as their eyes gazed into the branches of the trees over their heads. Nan followed their gaze and soon they were all staring at eyes staring back at them. Everywhere throughout the trees, white-plumed tails hung.

"Colobus Monkeys," Marc explained, realizing there were about a hundred right over their heads watching them, probably waiting to grab the food. They were so startled, they put the kids back in the car, packed up the picnic, and ate lunch while they drove. As they came to the lake, an otherworldly scene spread out before them. The pale blue water, as clear as glass, reflected the long pink legs of what looked like an elegant corps de ballet of birds. They graced the shoreline as if walking on tiptoes, the shell-like beaks extending from long flowing necks, their movement appearing as if it had been choreographed. Thousands upon thousands of pink flamingos were gathered as far as the eye could see. It was an incredible scene of God's wonder and beauty, and quite a day.

CHAPTER 11

One Hundred Beds

Sheshamane. Ethiopia, 1969

In addition to the hospital, there was a leper village of about seven hundred individuals on the mission station. Many of those begging in the streets of Addis Ababa were gathered up and brought to the SIM hospital for treatment. The people with leprosy were instructed not to return to Addis, but they had to go back since begging was how they lived. The hospital had one hundred beds but was always overflowing with at least two hundred patients. There were people on the beds, between the beds, beneath the beds, as if camping out wherever they could find a spot to sit or rest their head. There was a shortage of nursing care, so families would come along with their sick family members to bathe them and cook for them. They brought along their own potties and cooking pots, walking miles and miles. Those that could not walk often arrived in wheelbarrows, with a family member walking behind, slowly rolling the patient. There were five different people groups in the hospital, so five different languages had to be translated for Marc as he worked.

As the people traveled through the mountains during the

cold nights to bring their sick to the hospital, they used long pieces of fabric to wrap themselves to stay warm. The colder it got, the more fabric they wrapped. When they arrived at the hospital, it all had to be removed. The dirt and bugs would fall out, diseases were exposed, and the smell at times was almost unbearable. Work days were sixteen hours long. Marc came home for dinner, and afterwards, when the kids were in bed, Nancy would sometimes go with him to make his night rounds. They stood at the doorway of the large room overflowing with sickness and disease, finding the whites of all the terrified eyes staring at them. Their hearts were so drawn to these people that they didn't realize at first how often the bugs brought by the patients were affecting Nancy. She was more sensitive to them than Marc and often woke up with eyes swollen shut and a face quite distorted.

One night, a man with a distended stomach that made him look nine months pregnant was brought in. No one knew what his condition was, but Dr. Hicks could tell the growth inside of him had to be removed. Nancy asked to observe the surgery, and a guard at the compound agreed to sleep in front of their house in case one of the kids woke up. Not long after they had left for the hospital, Paul woke up and went wandering out, calling, "Mama, Mama?" The guard, who was at least 6' 5", had dozed off under an army blanket. He suddenly jumped up. Paul saw the blanket fly like a cape and only the whites of the man's eyes. The guard grabbed Paul and ran with him to the hospital to find Nan. She recognized the screaming and left the operating room to comfort Paul while the guard was trying to explain the story. His eyes were as big as saucers, and as one of the nurses translated what he was saying to her, he kept repeating, "You can't leave these kids alone because of the hyenas!" But she didn't know. The hyenas stalking their house could have easily snatched up one of the children and killed them. Every day, they were even more aware of God's protection!

The surgery began. When Dr. Hicks opened the abdomen, they discovered huge cysts from the sheep tapeworm. Dissecting the tumor was very difficult because there were so many adhesions, and they couldn't afford to puncture the tumor. If it broke and the fluid ran into the man's abdomen, he would die immediately of anaphylactic shock. In fact, they would all be in danger. So with Marc on one side of the table and Dr. Hicks on the other and Nancy looking on, they removed a very fragile tumor the size of a basketball, so transparent, "you could see things swimming inside." Dr. Hicks was able to remove the tumor without breaking it, then discovered seven more cysts in the man's abdomen and chest cavity. He removed them all. The tumor was so unusual, they weighed, measured, and photographed it, later writing up an article to be published in the medical journals. Marc knew he was in the presence of a very great surgeon.

~

While Marc had still been in medical school at the University of Washington, Dr. Lindsay McClenny came to speak to the Christian medical students. He was a scholar, very humble, and the head of the SIM hospital in Shashamane. He had also been connected to the University Presbyterian Church in Seattle and was one of the greatest people Marc had ever met. Dr. McClenny lived to serve people. He had worked in the Sudan and Yemen before coming to Ethiopia, and Marc had been particularly impacted by his story of the day the Sudanese Army showed up at his village, demanding the doctor leave everything and be gone within twenty-four hours. Dr. McClenny had come to love the people he served there, and the thought of not knowing what would happen to them was almost unbearable. As he drove out of the village, the people all came running toward him, gathered around him, and told him they had decided to follow Jesus.

Some of the greatest suffering Marc had ever seen happened in Shashamane. Marc admitted one very frightened woman to the hospital with such sores on her face that it was hard to tell if she was even human. During rounds, he was told to get her out right away. She had anthrax, a highly contagious disease, but Marc didn't know that. She was put in isolation, and they fought for her life for five days but without success.

Birth complications were especially common in the poor areas of the mountains. One day, a married couple came to see Marc, and it was apparent to him how much this young husband loved his wife. They were about eighteen years old and arrived all dressed up in their wedding clothes because they wanted to be treated well. The wife had been in labor for days, unable to deliver the baby, and large parts of her body had already died. No one knew what to do. There was a specialist in Addis who could try to help her, so that's where they sent her. But the baby was stillborn.

There were extraordinary issues with abnormal births. Prenatal care was almost nonexistent. Malnutrition caused many stillbirths. Other times, the way the baby entered the birth canal was a problem. All that was needed was a single person who could have reached in and turned the head, and a lot of lives could have been saved. God certainly cares for these mission hospitals. "These mission doctors and nurses walk right into the pain and suffering of the world for Jesus' sake."

Dr. McClenny's two daughters attended school in Addis and wanted to take Nancy there to show her the market area. She was all eyes and told them she would love to go. So they traveled together to Addis. While shopping in the huge open market, they heard a gunshot. The girls took off running, yelling for her to run. She didn't know where to run to, and her only thought was, "Why?" She lost them, and there she was in a crowded market, people running in all directions, screaming and yelling, and she felt as if she'd lost the only connection she had to Earth. When they finally reconnected, Nancy cried.

"Why did you abandon me?"

"If someone is shot, we would be blamed because we are the foreigners. We had to get out of there as fast as we could, or we would be the guilty ones no matter what!" Nancy felt so naive, but she learned about the scapegoat concept.

CHAPTER 12

Give Me the Keys to the Car

"Stay alert! I am God, the God of everything living.
Is there anything I can't do?"
(Jeremiah 32:27, MSG)

Shashamane, Ethiopia, 1969

Early morning mist hovered, the moon, milky white, faded as the sun rose, silhouetting the trees' angular branches, twisting and jutting out while bullfrogs sat in a night's collection of foam. A shimmer of rose-colored hues slowly covered the golden-green grasslands. Egyptian geese traveled to their waterhole as brave ducklings hidden in a tree jumped down one by one to follow, scampering forward into unknown territory, trusting their parents.

Chameleons sauntered. Dung beetles rolled their prize balls. One lone duckling scurried beneath a bird's dazzling red and turquoise wings. Turtles maneuvered a pool party of elephants. Marc would rise each morning at five to cross the large grassy field and gather with the rest of the staff to pray at Dr. McClenny's house before the day began. Later in the day, sticky flies would turn his shirt pure black, but the early morning hours were wondrous.

The elevation and cold would make it hard to get out of bed, and one morning, Marc was so tired, he just didn't want to get up. But he felt God speak to him. He rose and started out for the prayer meeting. When he reached the field, God spoke to him, quoting from Jeremiah, saying, "I am the Lord. I made the heavens and the earth, is there anything too hard for me?" No, Lord! And then God stopped him again at the far end of the field, repeating the same words. Marc stopped and answered, "No, Lord, I don't think anything is too hard for you." But he also got really scared because he wondered why God was telling him that. He went on into Dr. McClenny's house, and everyone told him that he and Nancy would be staying in Shashamane for the long haul. The missionaries alerted Marc that there had been a revolution in Somalia the night before, the president had been assassinated, the Russian military had taken over the country, the Communists had control of everything, and the airport had been shut down. The entire parliament had been put in prison. There was no TV and no way of hearing news without others that were "connected."

He listened as the hospital staff told Marc again that he wouldn't be able to get into Somalia. But Marc now realized nothing was too hard for God. He didn't know how to tell them; he had received a Word from God that he was supposed to go. He was sure they thought he was just a Pentecostal crazy kid who didn't want to listen to them. But he was determined to follow through on God's call, and so he needed to drive to Addis to get Somali visas stamped in their passports. Finally, he convinced them to lend him a car.

The road to Addis was close to the hospital, Marc knew that road because of the many devastating car accidents he was treating at the hospital. And he knew you didn't want to be on that road at night. In many places there were no shoulders. If you tried to pull over, you would go off the cliff. So at nightfall, in order to rest, truck drivers would just stop wherever they were on the road. They would put a boulder behind the truck, another one in front, and sleep underneath. There was one car accident after another. Marc had never seen so much trauma anywhere as he experienced from those accidents.

He started out, driving until he reached the edge of the Rift Valley which went all the way down from the Red Sea in Israel, through the Great Lakes region of Africa where the two tectonic plates met. Suddenly traffic stopped. There were bumper-to-bumper cars about a mile long all the way down into the Valley, down both sides of the road. In the middle of all these cars was a Nigerian oil company (AGIP) truck with gas bottles burning. AIGP sold bottled gas all across Africa. He got out and asked what was going on and was told that the truck was about to explode. They were all just waiting until it happened then they would move on. Marc talked to the Lord.

"I'm thinking that You made heaven and earth, and there isn't anything too hard for You. So I'm just going to drive down there, if it's okay with You." Marc drove on, waving at everybody as he passed, right on past the AIGP gas truck, to the other side and arrived in Addis before nightfall, which was a good thing.

There Marc met John Cumbers, a very kind man, who had an understanding of Africans and missionaries. He was in charge of the mission office in Addis Ababa and oversaw SIM in all of Ethiopia. He had been in the British Army in Iraq for years, and he had also been a circus clown at one time. He knew the area really well and could have just laughed at Marc when he said he was going to the Somali embassy. Instead, first he told him he didn't think he would be able to get into Somalia. Second, he said that because Africans are very relational, they don't like to say no to people, so instead of saying no, they just won't do anything. He told him to bring a book along to read during the day, and at the end of the day, when they hadn't done anything, he would pick Marc up.

"Do you have your book?" John asked Marc as he drove up to the Embassy. Marc nodded. John told him that he knew the ambassador and would go in with him to talk to him. He pulled up and parked the car, and Marc walked in with him carrying his book and their passports. As they started making their way to the back of the Embassy, the Ambassador saw them and came running, grabbed John, and gave him a big hug. When he saw all the passports in Marc's hand, he grabbed them and gave them to his secretary. And just like that, they got their visas. The Ambassador told Marc the last plane into Somalia would be leaving the next day. "If you want to be on it, be there." Then he looked at Marc and smiled. "You're going to really like Bulo Burte. The wind never stops blowing there."

Marc had to turn around and drive straight back to Shashamane during the night, on that same treacherous road that you weren't supposed to be on after dark. Early the next morning, he raced into the house, telling Nancy to hurry. They had to leave in ten minutes. So after six weeks of settling into life in Shashamane, Nancy had to pack everything, clean, put things in place, and prepare the children for travel. In ten minutes. And she did. During that time, Marc took care of wrapping things up at the hospital.

"Are you really taking your family there? Seriously?" The stunned staff looked at him. "There's a war! No one can get in!" Because they were such kind people, they'd been avoiding talking to Marc about his plans. They thought there had to have been some big mistake and Marc and his family would end up right in the middle of that war. But they didn't say anything after that. They just didn't know what to say.

Early that morning, on the same treacherous road, just as the sun cracked its radiant light through the dark sky beyond the mountains, the family drove back to Addis. They boarded a small plane with the Ambassador who was returning to his country and flew into Somalia on what was to be the last flight in for a long time. If God hadn't talked to Marc, they would have never arrived in Somalia. But on arrival it was difficult not to wonder if he had made the right decision. When they got off the plane, it was a hundred-ten degrees. Oh my goodness, it was hot!

CHAPTER 13

The Land of the Poets

*"He turned the desert into pools of water and the
parched ground into flowing springs."
(Psalm 107:35, NIV)*

Mogadishu, Somalia, 1969

Samuel Francis Burton, an explorer in the middle of the
19th century, wrote these words about Somalia in his book,
First Footsteps in East Africa, page 91.

"The country teems with poets... every man has his
recognized position in literature as accurately defined as
though he had been reviewed in a century of magazines—
the fine ear of this people causing them to take the greatest
pleasure in harmonious sounds and poetic expressions..."

An essential understanding of the power structure of the
country of Somalia is that the real leaders are all poets. Somalis
are great orators, and they love to talk. When the opposition
to the Communists began to rise up, Somali leaders put
together theatre groups to perform poetry readings. When
they arrived in Bulo Burte, people were talking about how
great one of the readings had been. That group of Somali
performers had continued on to the next village when the

government came and killed them all. They realized the poets were making fun of the government through poetry. This was the climate they had stepped into.

Somalis are a beautiful people dating back to one of the oldest people groups in the world—their culture dates back four thousand years. Families are proud of their heritage and memorize the names of their ancestors. They know family names back many generations in order to remind themselves of who they are. If they were from corrupt people, they'd just say they didn't remember, to cover up. If people didn't know their genealogy, they were considered horse thieves who must be hiding something, or they were orphans. Nobility knew their heritage, whereas peasants might not, which is typical of nomadic cultures. The Somalis would ask Marc about his family. He only knew back to his great-grandfather, Sandy McBain. He and his friend, Jack, pioneered a town in Ontario. Jack had a strong faith, but Sandy wanted nothing to do with that. On Saturday nights, he enjoyed playing his fiddle for all the parties in the neighborhood. (The following excerpt is from *The Hand of the Potter* by Marc's mother, Delnora M. Erickson.)

"I finished with religion a long time ago," said Sandy. "You're wasting your words. I have no faith at all."

"No one has faith until God plants it in his heart," said his friend Jack.

"Then it hasn't been planted in mine," said Sandy gruffly. "I feel no stirrings of it."

"You're a stubborn Scotchman," said Jack. "If you'd give God half a chance, He could make a new person of you."

"Oh?" said Sandy with a broad smile. "Maybe I'm satisfied the way I am. Who would be wanting to make over Sandy McBain?"

In an attempt to get his friend to be quiet, Sandy went to church with him one Sunday.

That Sunday, the preacher asked the congregation, "Does the love of God mean nothing to you? Can you scoff at the truth that God's Son laid down His own life to save your soul? Can you turn your back on that kind of love and tell yourself that it doesn't matter?"

Sandy thought the preacher was speaking directly to him, and he got mad at Jack talking to the preacher about him. But Jack hadn't said anything. After that, the two went in different directions. But the preacher's words, "Does it mean nothing to you that God loves you?" kept returning to him.

One day he went into the forest to cut wood, and he saw a white figure standing where a tree he'd cut down had stood. The eyes of the stranger went straight through him. He dropped his ax, his knees buckled, the compassion he saw in the eyes looking at him unnerved him. He covered his face and lay on the ground. When he was able to look up again, the figure was gone. All he could remember were the words, "Isn't my love enough?"

When Saturday night came, Sandy took out his violin and instead of going to the party, he played songs his mother had taught him, songs she used to sing to him so he could fall asleep as a child. That night, he felt a battle pass. He took the violin and nailed it to the wall.

After that, his quick temper subsided, along with a lot

of drunken fights. He started to spend a lot of time with the Bible. He wanted to learn more, but there was a problem. He couldn't read. Then he met Harriet Bagsley who helped him learn. They fell in love and got married.

And now Marc and Nancy would help the Somalis learn about the Bible and how to read.

The Somalis knew much about life from living in the desert. Because they were a nomadic people, nobody really knew them that well. They would come down into the trading centers to sell their cattle and wares. They moved back and forth. If there wasn't any rain, they went to the village wells to survive. But their culture was really strong. For about five hundred years of their history, they were Jewish. Remember the Queen of Sheba? She was probably Somali. They later became Christians, for centuries. It wasn't until about the fourteenth century that all of the Christians were killed. This is documented by studying the names of generations past.

The poets heard God speaking to them, and the poets led. Somali news, history, and family stories were told in poems because that was how it could be remembered. It was similar to putting words to music when you want children to learn. It was like the book of Proverbs. They held onto their proverbs and stories this way.

There was no Somali alphabet in 1969, no script. Before anything could be put into print, this needed to be agreed on by the Somali government. Missionaries were using Roman script to write words and proverbs as they heard them. Warren and Dorothy Modrickers were pioneer missionaries to the Somalis in 1956. They had lived previously for a long time in Aden (Yemen) before coming to Mogadishu to learn Somali and translate the Scriptures. The first translation of the New Testament into Somali wasn't completed until 1979. The Gospel of Luke was the first to be translated into Somali by using phonetics. An official Somali script wasn't declared until 1982. Finally, the New Testament could be put in print.

The people in the village didn't speak perfect Somali. It was a blend of Italian, Arabic, and all kinds of dialects. The people from the bush, the nomads of the desert, spoke pure Somali, and it was musical to hear. They were all poets. If you weren't a poet and didn't know the language, you didn't have a chance with the people from the bush. So that was what the Modrickers had to work around in translating the Gospel. After the script was made official, the next hurdle was teaching people to read their language.

~

Having landed at the airport in Mogadishu, Marc realized there had been no communication from the mission about their coming. What he didn't know was that the missionaries in Mogadishu had been going back and forth to the airport, expecting them for the past six weeks. They had decided on that very day that it would be the last time they were going to look for them. The family was either going to be there or they would not go back. And then they found them.

It was quite an arrival. There they were with four kids. Marc still had Lisa on his back in the gerry-pack. He was wearing a light blue cotton suit coat, and Lisa had wet through her diaper and soaked his back. "Take this baby, take this baby! Do something!" he said. They went into the central building at the airport on the main floor, where there was a balcony of people looking down on them. There was no restroom, and there was no place to go. You couldn't get out of line, and he kept saying, "Take this baby!" Nancy couldn't get to a diaper. She couldn't go anywhere. She had to grin and bear it. And so did Marc.

Howard Borlase and a young Australian named John Warner from the missionary headquarters picked them up at the airport. They took the family to headquarters, where they were given a meal around one p.m. They put the kids down for a rest and were told that someone would take them grocery shopping. That was a cross-cultural experience. It was their first in Africa.

After the rest hour, garage doors were heard being pulled up to create hundreds of kiosks along the sandy streets of the market. They were told to buy enough food for six people for six weeks. It was hard to imagine what they would need for six weeks. Nancy wondered as she walked into the claustrophobic space, confronted with three walls of floor-to-ceiling shelves loaded with cans of food. They had never lived on canned food. How many would they need? The labels weren't in English. You had to shop by the picture. All her tired mind could think of was what kind of a meal could she make out of this? How many meals would it cover? What would she do if they ran out? How many rolls of toilet paper did they need? She looked at the pictures and made a good guess: four of these and five of those. She just had to start buying. If she didn't find something in one store, she walked to the next kiosk and began again. Later, she found out you couldn't trust the pictures. You'd think you were opening a can of green beans and find grape jelly. She'd never seen canned corn beef. The kids thought it was dreadful. She served it once and never again. Nine cans of it were left on the shelf.

There were no grocery carts. As she chose things, the merchant would write up a tab. Marc would pay and carry things to the car, load by load. The Suez Canal was closed that year, so all shipping had to go down around Cape Horn, the southern tip of Africa. Mogadishu was the last seaport coming from both the East and the West. Whatever was left on the ship had to be sold in Mogadishu. Everything had to be sold there. The merchant may say he just wanted certain goods, but the ship captain would offer all or nothing, so he could go home empty or reload something else for the return trip. The merchants often didn't know exactly what they were buying. The canned goods came from countries all around the world with labels in languages they couldn't read.

At headquarters for the evening meal, Howard shouted, "One of your kids stepped on a stink ant!" A terrible odor filled the room. Howard was a very proper Canadian, and he and his wife had no children of their own. The Erickson boys thought Howard would be embarrassed to know that he had ants in his house. They thought they were doing Howard a favor by stepping on them.

Finally, the car was loaded with three adults, four kids, all the suitcases, and six weeks' worth of groceries. They took off at ten p.m. and drove through the night on Victory Road to Bulo Burte. Mussolini had built the "highway" sixty years earlier. When WWII started, the Italians invaded Somalia and Ethiopia, and Somalia became an Italian colony. That's how the road came by that name. The problem, however, was that no one had repaired the road since. It was full of huge potholes the entire trip. They drove down one side of the pothole and out the other. Seven hours later, they arrived at the mission station in Bulo Burte. It had been a very long day.

CHAPTER 14

The Dusty City

"What is required of a Missionary of Charity is this:
health of mind and body, ability to learn, a good dose
of good sense, and a joyous character."
— *Mother Teresa*

Bulo Burte, Somalia 1969

Left behind was the lush tropical rain forest with its huge lakes—all mountains and wild jungle—a place where flamingos migrated. If you ever wanted to get a feel for Africa, Shashamane was the place to go. Bulo Burte was all desert and dust. When Marc stepped out of the car onto the golden earth, he said, "I've never been anywhere in my entire life that is so much like no place in particular." Was that another way to say "boring?"

The land was board-flat with dust everywhere. Not a mountain anywhere off in the distance to be seen, not even a single hill. It was like standing on a huge tabletop. It was the way most deserts seem when you first get there. But by the time you leave, you've realized it was full of life, full of beauty. But it took a while to learn and to get over the culture shock. Maybe you never really do.

Marc was sent to cover for Dr. Joanne Adair at the SIM Hospital in Bulo Burte. She left for Australia just two days after they arrived to take an extended leave. A doctor needed nurses and backup help that were well trained, and auxiliary people to help for safety, so there were five women nurses on the compound—Joy, Marlene, Mary, Anne, and Ruth—that staffed the hospital. Ruth was the only married nurse. Her husband took care of the machinery and the buildings.

There was a cement block house ready for the Ericksons on the mission station to settle into. It had two bedrooms, a little living/dining area, and a kitchen with a charcoal stove. To welcome them, the missionaries had added a shower and indoor toilet because they had heard about the four children coming. Marc and Nancy were the only people on the compound to have indoor plumbing. Nan was thrilled with the improvements to welcome them.

It was so dry, there weren't even any rats. The houses in the village were made with stick frames with dirt floors. They were made out of limbs of brush tightly woven with vines, then packed with mud and sometimes whitewashed. The same sticks were used to make a fence around the house, creating what was referred to as a "compound." Inside, the children played, the chickens and the goat or whatever they owned roamed freely. The closer you got to the center of town, more of the houses were square and sometimes made out of a combination of cement block and sticks and mud, all whitewashed.

The cooking fire was usually outside the little house, where four to six women might be sitting on camel stools—

little low stools made with stout stick legs and a piece of camel hide stretched for the seat. There they would peel their garlic, stir the fire, and start a meal. It had a communal feel with the women and children, working and visiting together.

Daughters were mothers' helpers and mostly out of sight. Before the age of marriage, they were always in their compounds with their mothers. The young boys were free and usually running through the village. They were called 'market boys' because they were always getting into trouble in the market. They would swipe things from whomever was trying to sell something, or they would throw stones at the new arrivals because they were outsiders. But they liked to play with the Erickson boys and were very inventive. They cut barbed wire off the mission compound fence to make little cars with long handles and parade them around.

The small, very rural town had a total population of about twenty thousand. Houses in the town center sat right alongside the streets. The walls of the courtyards faced in, creating narrow lanes with a doorway into each yard. Sometimes, bulls would come running through, leaving you no place to go. One day, Paul had gone into town with some friends and had fallen behind. All of a sudden, he heard a bull behind him. He was not going to let it outrun him, so he started to take off when a woman reached out of one of the little openings, grabbed him, and pulled him into her house. When they got home that day, the twins told their mom they had almost lost Paul. For the next six weeks, Paul kept saying, "That lady saved my life! She saved my life!" He was only three years old. He loved to talk and was often called the little orator.

~

There was a period of adjustment, as there always is, both for those already there and for those coming in. The missionaries on the compound were either English or Australian and not especially enamored with Americans. It wasn't their fault. It had just been their previous experience. Marc and Nancy were young, with four little kids that were needy. They didn't know the language. They had nothing they could bring but Jesus. They knew He was in them, and in their weakness, He would be strong. God had to make them strong, or how could they have stayed in the desert in East Africa?

There were dangers all around them: snakes, wild animals, clans fighting, and a government law against Christianity. And there was a revolution going on, the Russian takeover. Fourteen different Oppositional Somali clans passed their village regularly. They didn't really have protection. There were unknowns and challenges, and misunderstandings and cross-cultural differences that, each day, hit them in the face and made them wonder if they would ever be able to relate.

The first month or two, the nurses were often frustrated with them. Their weaknesses were apparent. It was curious to them why they would be sent when they had their hands full with their own lives and family. It was obvious to Marc and Nancy that the missionaries had been pouring out all they had. They were tired. Their "can do" enthusiasm and "wanting to change the world" attitude, "believing God was going to do it through them" approach was like putting salt on a wound. The missionaries all knew the language, they had been there for years, they had taken care of every family in the village. Marc and Nan began to feel as though everyone would be happier if they just left.

They had to close their door and pray, "We can do nothing." They needed reminding every day, it was Christ in them that was going to make a difference. It wasn't about them. Nancy would think about how Marc was the one with the education, that's what was needed. Who was she? Nothing. Who were her kids? Excess baggage.

There were no other children around the compound, and the missionaries wanted the Erickson children to behave like adults. The one family there had sent their own daughter to Addis to go to school. She was the same age as the twins. Nancy had offered to educate her along with their boys. But the girl's parents refused, even though she was only in kindergarten. So they never got to see her much at all. She eventually ended up having to repeat that year because she was so homesick being away from her parents. She wasn't ready to handle the experience. The missionaries often joked that SIM stood for, Sure I'll Move. They moved all the time, and it took its toll on them. They were tired.

The missionaries were very disciplined people of prayer. Being American seemed to rub them the wrong way. They had been through many difficult things. The nurses were respectful and kind, but it seemed as though they had lost hope that anything could happen fast. They needed encouragement, but at times, it seemed to Marc and Nancy that they were a stone in their shoes. They were up against an old-guard mission mentality. They had good relationships, but it began to feel as though they were pulling the plow in opposite directions—you can't, yes you can, we can't, yes we can.

But in spite of it all, the Erickson house was always open to visitors and guests.

CHAPTER 15

Basketball, Books and a Trip to the Beach

"Sweet are the uses of adversity which like the toad, ugly and venomous, wears yet a precious jewel in his head; and this our life, exempt from public haunt, finds tongues in trees, books in the running brooks, sermons in stones, and good in everything"
— *William Shakespeare*

Bulo Burte, Somalia 1969

Marc had just come from one of the busiest hospitals in all of Africa in Shashamane. The nurses in Bulo Burte were all midwives and handled most deliveries, and the climate was healthier. Marc could help with infectious diseases, snake bites, broken bones, and other emergencies. He made rounds on every patient twice a day, but he and Nancy wondered what kind of ministry they could help with. The staff explained to him that there were only two Christians in the entire village of twenty thousand, so there wouldn't be much for him to do spiritually. They sent a prayer letter out telling people to pray for the doctor in Somalia. "Pray that he will get used to the slow pace!"

Marc found clay soil on the compound and decided to build a tennis court. After hours of hauling clay during rest hours every day and making a cement roller to smooth the surface, and hiring someone to make a net, they gave it a try. But with no fences, they spent all their time chasing balls. So after procuring two trees from a truck that arrived from Ethiopia, and reshaping two rims for basketball hoops, it became a basketball court. Every night from four to six o'clock, Marc played basketball with the young men of the village. That was to become the cornerstone of their ministry. Since there was nothing else for them to do, all the young men between the ages of fifteen and twenty-five would gather and line up to play. Afterward, Marc would invite them over to read the New Testament and work on their English. Two-thirds of them wouldn't come because they were afraid to read the Bible. But for those who did come, Nancy would serve limeade and cookies for the Bible study.

Everything changed when the lead nurse, Joy Newcomb, an Australian Obstetrics (OB) nurse, returned from furlough. She had been praying for ten years for someone to come and help the young men of the village. She had delivered most of the babies in the village for over a decade, even before the hospital was built. She would take a piece of linoleum, rubbing alcohol, and a razor blade and go into their homes for delivery. She loved everybody there and knew everyone by name. Someone let her know that Marc had been praying for one of the teenage drug dealers named Abdi. He was considered so dangerous that he wasn't allowed to go to school anymore. He was one of the guys in the desert that would steal for drug money and ride the trucks all the way down to South Africa. When she asked about him, Marc told her Abdi had given his life to Jesus. So Joy went off to see him, and when she came back, she said, 'Marc, Abdi is a Christian! You saved him. I don't know what's going on here, but you keep playing basketball with these kids.' She told him to just keep doing what he was doing, and she would run the hospital. If there was something she couldn't handle, she would come for him. Otherwise, 'keep working with these kids!'

But when Marc was told by the mission that he couldn't baptize anyone, he realized they wouldn't be able to stay there. "The Great Commission in the twenty-eighth chapter of the Book of Matthew, verses 18 through 20, is pretty clear on that," he said. He had brought his family ten thousand miles from home, sold everything, didn't have any place to go back to, and then he found out he wasn't going to be allowed to baptize believers! The government had shut that down. In addition, if anyone wanted to know about Jesus, the missionaries had agreed to make that person put in writing that they had initiated the conversation, then file that statement with the government. The chances weren't likely that someone would write a letter explaining they wanted to know about Christ. It was against their culture, and they could end up in prison. The mission had caved in to these government demands, afraid of being kicked out and losing their investment. "But didn't Jesus say, unless you were willing to forsake all, you couldn't be His disciple?" Marc let the mission know he would stay and cover for them until their doctor, JoAnne Adair, returned, but he couldn't stay without being obedient to the Great Commission. He was committed to making disciples.

The Russians were pushing communism on the kids wherever they went. The community appreciated Marc's medical help and was willing to stretch the boundaries a little in applying the government stipulations, but Marc knew in his heart they wouldn't be staying in Bulo Burte long-term. The plan had changed.

~

Some of the young villagers who played basketball had a little bit of Gospel teaching from years before and had become secret believers. When they came to the Ericksons' house to read with Nancy, they would often talk about a man named Brian Moray. He had started a school at one time through SIM in Bulo Burte, and kids stayed in a dorm which he oversaw. He taught them all kinds of Scripture verses and songs like, " This Little Light of Mine." They liked Brian a lot and told Nancy when they misbehaved, Brian was not afraid to spank them. She asked them if that bothered them and they said it didn't because they knew they needed it. The chiefs and fathers felt differently, but the boys knew how much Brian cared about them. When the boys were really bad, Brian would discipline them. He ran the school for several years, but because it was Christian, the government came and had it shut down. Any of the students that finished primary school could go to Mogadishu for high school, where there were four high schools for them to choose from. But by the time Marc and Nan had arrived in Bulo Burte, the mission school had closed.

After the school closed, Brian went up into Ethiopia to work at the mission headquarters. The mission office didn't give him much to do; he was sent on errands and picked up missionaries at the airport. Ten years later, Marc was in Addis Ababa and Brian picked him up at the airport. Marc was able to tell Brian about the many, many people in Bulo Burte who had come to faith. He told Brian that he had been the one to plant those good seeds. He needed to know that. Brian stopped the car, pulled over, and started to cry. He felt his whole life had been a complete loss. Marc told him when we all get to heaven and we're standing around talking to the Lord about that, He'll say something like, "Okay, Brian, Marc's already told you what happened down there. You felt sorry for yourself for a few years. Although you couldn't see the fruit then, now you understand the work I had called you to. Thank you."

During this time, Nancy was teaching her six-year-old twins how to read. The children loved learning. The young men of the village who had never had any education would come and study alongside their boys. They would come and read, and the boys would help them sound out words or explain their meanings. They had brought along forty copies of Good News for Modern Man in English, a New Testament translation with line drawings illustrating the story. That helped them understand the Scripture. They could look at the pictures and figure out what the story was about. As they read a little, they wanted more.

Some of them began to come two and three times a day to ask if they could read. They would all sit in a circle on the floor. The twins were learning to sound out the words phonetically, and the men would do the same thing. Then they would stop and talk about it together. There was an interest in education and in getting ahead. The young men were in their twenties, but educationally, they were all at the same learning level.

Nancy had packed a drum of books for the kids to read because she thought they were going to be there long-term. She had collected hundreds and hundreds of little paperback books for different levels. She explained to the young men that it was a library, and of course, they could borrow them, but they didn't understand the concept of a lending library. All the books disappeared over time.

About every six weeks, the Ericksons drove back to Mogadishu to replenish supplies. They tried to make it a family outing to go to the Indian Ocean for a swim. The mission headquarters staff always had prayer time at three o'clock. On one particular day, after that long, hot seven-hour drive, Nancy told the kids if they took a nap, she would take them to the beach. While the others were at prayer, Nancy and the kids got in the car to go to the beach. They had only driven about a half block when a policeman blew his whistle and stopped her. He wanted her to get out of the car.

He didn't speak English, and she didn't speak Somali. He was yelling something at her, but she didn't know what.

He used hand motions that made her think he was going to arrest her. Then he told her to leave the car where it was, leave the children, and give him the keys. She was scared and told him she was going for help. She walked back to the mission and went into the prayer meeting to ask if there was someone who could help her speak Somali. They were firm: "No, it's prayer time, we can't help you." She went back, tears running down her cheeks, the car was still in the intersection with the kids, and the policeman was standing there waiting for her. She shook her head. "Nobody's coming." He laughed and left.

She got back in the car and drove away wondering what that was all about. She was shaken, but they went on and enjoyed a swim. Eventually, she forgot about it. Whatever it had been about, she hadn't understood that day.

CHAPTER 16

Yousef

"When one does not love too much, one does not love enough."
— *Blaise Pascal*

Bulo Burte, Somalia, 1970

If someone came to see Marc at the hospital, he always gave that person at least fifteen minutes, no matter who they were. As a missionary, you weren't supposed to talk about Christ or you could be put in jail because of the agreement with the governor. Remember? A letter had to be on file from that person. That didn't stop Marc.

One day he was trying to share the Gospel with one of his patients. The patient didn't know English and Marc didn't know enough Somali, so Marc tried to phonetically read from the Somali Gospel of John. The man obviously was not understanding. There was a young man named Yousef, who had been at the hospital for several months with serious tuberculosis (TB). He poked his head in.

"Hi." Yousef was a cartographer from the north, very wealthy and highly educated. But he had previously made it clear to Marc not to tell him anything about Jesus. He didn't want to hear a single word of it. As Yousef was growing a little stronger, he would walk around the compound. Yousef saw that Marc was trying to read to the patient from the Gospel of John, but wasn't communicating well. Marc asked Yousef if he could help him translate and he agreed. Marc began to explain the Gospel to the man and after about ten minutes of going back and forth, he realized that Yousef was speaking much more than he was. Marc found that interesting and asked Yousef why.

"This man doesn't understand the concept you're talking about," Yousef said. "I have to explain to him first what the concept is, then tell him what you're saying."

"Are you a believer of Jesus, Yousef?' Marc stopped what he was doing.

"Yes."

"When did that happen?" he asked, astonished.

"Just now!'"

Yousef's family was so wealthy, he paid his medical bill with one one-thousand-shilling note. He started coming to the Erickson's house and said he felt as though he had lived there all his life.

"I don't want to leave here," he said. "I feel like I'm home." He didn't want to go back to Hargeisa, the capital city in the Republic of Somaliland, where he was originally from. But when his family realized he had become a Christian, they took him south to Mogadishu to have him treated in the hospitals there.

He later died there. "But I know he's in heaven now!"

Marc said. To Marc, the wonderful thing that can happen to any human being on any given day is to be able to talk to God as you go through that day, and see how He changes everything. Just to be able to say, "Oh God, what did You just do?" is absolutely amazing to experience.

CHAPTER 17

Meeting Ahmed

*"When I believed in Christ so much became clear,
I knew where I had come from and where I was going"*
— Ahmed Haile

Bulo Burte, Somalia 1970

On Sunday mornings, all the mission staff would gather to listen to a sermon tape together. This frustrated Marc and Nancy. They longed for a more personal approach. Surely the missionaries were all mature believers, capable of speaking, digging in, sharing a more personal Word from God, and experiences from their lives with Christ. On the way home one Sunday, after listening to one more sermon tape, Marc was kicking at the ground.

"I don't want to go back to one of those stupid services," he quipped. "I don't like this. I want something alive. What's God doing here?" Their critical spirit didn't help. Neither of them was yet aware of how tired these dear ladies were, how thin they had been stretched waiting for help.

When they reached home, they sat down at the kitchen table and prayed together that God would bring them some Somalis to talk to and even one that could speak English.

Within half an hour, they heard a knock. Marc opened the door, and there stood two teenage men. One said, "Hello, I'm Ahmed Haile. This is my friend, Ali Nur. We want to become Christians." In Ahmed's left hand, he was holding a copy of The Origin of the Species. In his right, a dictionary. Marc and Nancy were suspicious. They tried to tell Ahmed and Ali every reason why they wouldn't want to be Christians. They could be killed, they would be kicked out of their family, they might not find a job. Surely the Ericksons didn't have the resources to get them to America or pay for their education. There were so many dangers involved. They thought if these young men were coming for any false reason, they wouldn't waste their time. But Ahmed and his friend kept saying none of those things mattered. They just wanted to know Christ. Finally, they shared the Good News of Jesus's death to save us. Marc knew the Holy Spirit was speaking and invited the two of them to pray, inviting Jesus to come and indwell them. And they did. Later, Ahmed wrote: "That day in Marc's home when we prayed together for the Holy Spirit to reveal Jesus Christ to me was the most important day of my life. Although I did not fully understand what it meant to believe in and follow Jesus, I knew that I had begun a journey of incredible challenge and purpose. That is the day I truly came home!"

"I realized again why God had stopped me that morning and asked if there was anything too hard for Him. He wanted to get me to Somalia to meet Ahmed. Ahmed had been waiting for me. He'd been asking everybody in his family to tell him about Issa (Jesus) in the Quran. Ahmed had become a Quranic teacher. He knew the Quran better than anyone in the family. But what he loved most from the Quran was the story of Jesus."

Ahmed kept coming back to the house. He often came three times a day when he was in Bulo Burte, and would always ask to read the Bible. So Nancy read with him. The kids would sit with him, going over the narrative word by word, running their fingers over the syllables. Years previously, when Ahmed was sick in the SIM hospital in Bulo Burte with malaria, the nurses had given him Bible stories from the Old Testament to read. The story of Joseph, the son of Jacob, piqued his curiosity. The story in the Bible gave much more information about the life of Joseph than the Quran. This started his desire to dig in deeper and read the Bible. One day, he asked Nancy, "What do the words, "Nothing but the blood of Jesus" mean?" Nancy explained the Cross and they talked through Jesus's sacrifice together.

Ahmed was attending high school in Mogadishu by this time, so he was only in Bulo Burte during school breaks. Because he was very politically active and effective, and loved his country and his people, the Somali Government could see his leadership qualities and offered him a scholarship to go to East Germany to be trained. They wanted leaders who were committed to the Communist ideology. This was a test of his new faith.

Marc never talked to him about politics, but he did tell him he thought Communism was a Christian heresy. It had high ideals but operated without the Word of God, and without the Holy Spirit's power. He told Ahmed he had to be really careful before going to East Germany. The government was offering many scholarships for students in Marxist universities, either in East Germany or in the Soviet Union. Many of Ahmed's friends were also offered scholarships. His best friend went to East Germany, but some aspects of the revolution troubled Ahmed. To him, the government made promises, but Christ changed lives. Siad Barre, the President of Somalia, was being called their "Victorious Father". Ahmed's friends told him the way to success and security in the Somali revolution was to accept the scholarship.

The government officials wanted Ahmed to be the man in charge of all the border crossings. This could have made him very rich. But Ahmed saw the choice clearly. It was either committing to a life with Christ, or buying into Siad Barre's Marxism. He listened carefully. He wanted to grow in his faith, and he didn't want to live life only for himself. He turned down the scholarship. This meant he could no longer stay in Somalia, so he fled south to Kenya. Ahmed traveled on foot through very dangerous territory, so frightened, he prayed the Lord's prayer constantly throughout the journey. He arrived in Nairobi, not knowing who he would find there. At the bus station, miraculously, he found a friend who reconnected him with David Shenk, who he had known from Somalia. David oversaw the Mennonite mission in East Africa. During the year he was in Nairobi, Ahmed finished his senior year of high school, grew in his faith, continued to study the Bible, participated in Christian community and worship. He served and made many connections, all things not possible to the same degree in Somalia. (David later co-authored Ahmed's life story, Teatime in Mogadishu.)

CHAPTER 18

A Cure for Cholera

"Even in literature and art, no man who bothers about originality will ever be original: whereas if you simply try to tell the truth (without caring twopence how often it has been told before) you will, nine times out of ten, become original without ever having noticed it. Give up yourself, and you will find your real self."
— *C.S. Lewis*

Bulo Burte, 1970

Throughout this time, the missionaries at the hospital were growing increasingly unhappy with Marc. Since the Suez Canal was closed, they weren't able to get supplies into their area of East Africa very easily. The hospital had to order IV fluids up to two years in advance because the transport was so unpredictable. They were down to their last liter of IV fluids with no news of the next shipment when a man named Ali Jesu, who was the head man in a city to the south of them, came into the hospital.

It was pretty clear the man had typhoid fever and was going to die. Marc told the nurses to give him the liter of fluid, but they told Marc they only used the fluids for children. Marc argued over the liter and told them to trust the Lord would find them some fluids as needed. They were really angry, but reluctantly gave it to him, and Ali lived. Every time the man came through town after that, he would stop to thank Marc for saving his life.

The next day, Marc got in his little VW bus and drove south to find fluids. Nobody had any. The last place he stopped was the Italian Pharmacy. He went in, and there were stacks of boxes filling up the place. He asked the pharmacist what all the boxes were filled with. The man opened up one box and pulled out a bottle of IV fluid. "See this?" The fluid was cloudy. Marc told him it was just sugar and would precipitate. It wouldn't dissolve, the fluid wouldn't look clear, but it wouldn't hurt anything. "You know that, and I know that, but nobody's going to buy this stuff from me. It's useless." So Marc asked if he would give the boxes of IV fluid to him. The pharmacist agreed, and Marc filled up his bus with the boxes. He had to make three trips as they replaced the one protected liter with three carloads full. That quieted the nurses down, but they still weren't happy with Marc. They told him he was just lucky.

The fluids were lifesavers, but they went quickly. They saved the empty bottles.

~

Cholera came through Somalia for the first time in recent history. Dr. Adair had left an apparatus to distill water suitable for making IV fluids, plus a pharmaceutical scale and pure sodium chloride. She had known it would be needed at the hospital someday. When Marc found it in the storage room, he knew what to do. He had heard a report that cholera was present in the southern Soviet Union. Troops were being sent to Somalia from that region, and he knew it wouldn't be long before cholera would be in Somalia. He figured they could make their own IV fluids; after all, he had been a chemistry major. When patients started flowing into the hospital, Nancy began distilling water, drop by drop.

On their flight to Africa, Marc had happened to pick up a medical journal to read on the plane. He'd read the latest research papers in the New England Journal of Medicine from the National Institute of Health, and learned about the groundbreaking work being done on cholera in Thailand. "By God's grace, what I read was exactly what we needed." The problem they discovered was that the cholera toxin paralyzed the cells so they couldn't recycle water back into the colon. It just ran out in diarrhea, causing patients to die of dehydration within hours. They made IV fluids with distilled water, adding salt to make normal saline.

They made oral rehydration fluids with sugar, potassium chloride, and boiled water also.

They made pitchers of the fluid as fast as they could.

They gave those who became ill sips of water from the pitchers or ran IV fluids into them. They had discovered that a few sips of water over several hours was all that was needed to save a life. It was a major discovery. "It was a miracle — God was at work. We heard that most of the villages around us were losing about seventy people a day, but in our village, we didn't lose anybody." This had never been done before. When cholera came through the village again twelve years later, they were ready for it. They had the supply of the oral hydration drink and the IV fluids that were needed.

The villagers were scared. They stopped drinking the river water and started boiling it. The hospital had to be closed to all but cholera patients.

"Here we were living in this sea of death, working night and day because so many had become sick. Our house would get so hot because we kept a charcoal fire going through the night to continue sterilizing. Then we'd work with patients during the day."

In the midst of all this, Nancy was pregnant.

CHAPTER 19

A Baby in the Desert?

"Don't tell me the moon is shining;
show me the glint of light on broken glass."
— *Anton Chekov*

Bulo Burte, 1970

What would her parents think? When Nan first discovered she was pregnant with their fifth child, she knew they would be worried about her having the baby in Africa, so she kept putting off telling them. Finally, Marc pressed in, "Stop stalling. Tell them!" He told her to go for a walk in the desert and talk to God about it. She wondered if walking out in the desert alone was safe, but she did it. She walked quite far as she talked to God. By the time she returned, she knew she was prepared to let her parents know. She was confident this was God's good gift. It took a month for a letter to go to the US and a reply to come back. As she predicted, her parents were nervous about the situation. They recommended she either come home to the States for delivery or go to Europe.

She assured them she had a personal physician to care for her. Having a child in Bulo Burte would bond them with all the people in the village. Other foreigners had either gone to Kenya or home for deliveries. But why not have the baby there? A lot of babies were born there.

As soon as her older sister in Washington D.C. heard the news of the pregnancy, she went to the National Institute of Health and asked for the anesthesia instruments used in delivery. She had two kits sent to make sure if one didn't get through in the mail, the other would, and that Nancy would have anesthesia for the birth. One kit made it through, and Marc agreed they would use it. However, the lidocaine he had to use in the apparatus was ten years out of date, so it was useless.

The day she went into labor, she had a birthday party for the twins. One of the things they did every birthday was invite everybody on the compound to come for supper. She made a meal, a birthday cake, and homemade ice cream. They didn't have any way of freezing ice, so she took pans of water to all the merchants in town with little freezers and asked them to freeze it for her overnight. Then she would pick the pans up in the afternoon the next day, come home, and put it in the crank ice cream maker. That was always the big treat.

That birthday, she had seen a recipe for a frozen custard with eggs in it. She thought this would be extra special, so she put the eggs in with everything else. All the missionaries were there for dinner, and as they were scooping out the ice cream that night, there were a bunch of yellow balls in the ice cream. The yolks had frozen before the cream, so they all had frozen yolks.

These parties were always a big production, including

buying live chickens, butchering, and cooking them. By the time everyone left, she was exhausted. Once everyone was gone, Marc made his evening rounds at the hospital and returned, saying the last cholera patient had just gone home and the delivery room was empty and clean. They would need to go there that night to have the baby. So she walked with him down to the hospital.

Set up in the "delivery room" was an old Formica kitchen table with stirrups welded to the end. A lightbulb hung overhead. When they walked in, it was dark. The generator was off. It went off every night at eight o'clock. So they sent people to find the guard to turn on the generator. But nobody could find the guard. By this time, Nancy was in hard labor.

"We've got to get the lights on, someone get the lights on!" Marc kept repeating.

Finally, the nurses came over and were trying to get a lantern lit, but no one could light it. Now Marc told Nan, "Just don't push, don't push!"

"Honey, when it comes to this point, I can't hold back," Nancy took charge.

Marc told the nurses they would name the baby after whoever could light the lantern. The nurses laughed while they were working, and finally as the baby burst through, the lantern came on. They had already decided, though, if they had a girl, they would name her Heidi Joy.

Joy had lit the lantern. And they took Heidi Joy home that night.

Nancy learned as she went along. She regularly had a group of women come and study the Bible with her at the house. Not long after Heidi was born, the women came up in the afternoon to have tea and to talk over Scripture with her. She had Heidi in her arms over her shoulder facing a mirror on the wall behind her. She was talking away, and watching all these women gesturing, 'No, no, no!' She didn't know what they were upset about. She learned, in their culture, it was taboo for a baby to look in a mirror. They went wild while she tried to tell them about Jesus. Some people also believed it was taboo to tell a girl she was beautiful for fear it would make her vain and superficial.

When the girls in the village became marriageable age, the family arranged marriages for them. It was usually to somebody in their clan who would take good care of their daughter. That could be a painful time. Sometimes the girl knew the young man, or sometimes she'd never met him and didn't know the family. The Ericksons had a lovely girl named Sofia who came to help Nancy. She noticed one day Sofia's face had broken out everywhere and she asked the girl if something was wrong. Sofia told her that her parents had made an arrangement for her marriage. Nancy asked if she was happy about it.

"No, I don't know him." Sofia cried. She didn't want to marry him.

She was a believer, and she knew the chances of him being a Christian were zero. Nancy prayed with her and tried to counsel her to trust God, but she was so worked up, Nancy couldn't calm her. Supposedly, when you were married in that culture, you were given six months off work with pay to build your marriage. If you were to get pregnant, then you would get an additional six months off. Sofia got married, they paid her six months' salary, then she was pregnant, and they paid her six months more. While all that year she wasn't able to provide any help for Nancy. Obviously, most women didn't work outside the home. In the end, it worked out pretty well for Sofia. The man she married was open to her beliefs, loved, and cared for her. Years later, when they returned to Bulo Burte, Sofia came to Nancy to tell her all was well. God had heard her prayers.

In Islam, it was acceptable to have four wives at a time. Women had no rights. If a husband was unhappy with his wife, he only had to declare, "I divorce you." Then the woman had to return to her family, and the father kept her children. They knew one older man who had had twenty-six wives. The broken hearts of the children who had lost their mothers and the mothers who had lost their children at some point in their lives were unbelievable. There was a tremendous sense of loss and few happy marriages. Women were powerless.

CHAPTER 20

Dahir, Dorothy, and Desert Dangers

*"Courage is not the absence of fear but rather
the assessment that something else is more important
than fear."*
— *Franklin D. Roosevelt*

Bulo Burte, 1970

The Webi Shabeelle River flowed through Somalia, and the Somalis built little pumps to irrigate the area along the riverbanks. There was food in that area—mangos, cherry tomatoes, corn, green beans—but there was never much at the market.

One of the village kids named Dahir lived along the river. He would sneak food off his family's farm to bring for breakfast with the Erickson family. One day, after giving his life to Christ and subsequently being kicked out by his family, he came to live with them.

There were few groceries available, but Nancy enjoyed learning how to become an ever more creative cook. Once every six weeks, the family went to Mogadishu and stocked up on whatever she could find there. She learned to mix things up, trying to make something different out of the ordinary things they had. Spaghetti, rice, tomato paste, chickens, and eggs were usually available locally. But flour, sugar, milk powder, and butter came from Mogadishu. Instead of being picky eaters, the kids grew up saying how good the food was. They would think it was incredible she could make so many different things out of such a limited number of ingredients. She always felt thanked. Some Somalis would come regularly to eat with the family, but just when they were getting used to one thing, she'd serve something different. The Somalis liked sameness, and the Americans liked variety. But they always had a houseful. People loved being at their house.

If there were unexpected company, she had to be creative because there wasn't any local store to run to. Nancy's Aunt Dorothy was traveling around the world with her sister Pearl and had implied she might come for a visit one day. The sisters were in Nairobi when Dorothy sent a telegram to Somalia to tell of her upcoming visit. Later, she caught a flight to Mogadishu. On arrival, when no one was at the airport to pick her up, she assumed they hadn't received her message. Undaunted, Dorothy took a cab to the SIM headquarters and introduced herself. Howard Borlais and his wife, who had been the welcome party to greet the Ericksons when they first arrived and were in charge of the Somali ministry, asked if she could wait until they finished teaching their last class for the day at ten p.m. They would then drive her to Bulo Burte themselves. Howard was in his sixties and drove all through the night to bring Aunt Dorothy upcountry. At six AM there was a knock on the door. Marc went to answer it, assuming it was the hospital.

"Aunt Dorothy!" Nancy heard him say and leapt out of bed to run to her.

Sofia came that day, and Nancy sent her to get chickens and tell the ladies in the village that her aunt had arrived. They were going to have a party!

Sofia could hold a knife between her toes and, grabbing the head and feet of the chicken, cut off its head. That was the Somali way. But Sofia wanted to go home to dress for the party, and Nancy had to butcher her first chickens, pluck and cook them. She had watched it being done before. Paul especially loved to watch. Wide-eyed, he'd sit outside with his thumb in his mouth as Sofia put the butcher knife between her toes so she'd have both hands free to cut the head quickly. He was fascinated and would come inside so excited because Sofia was able to use her toes and have free hands.

That day Paul came running to her. "Mom, put the knife between your toes, put the knife between your toes, Mom!" But she didn't have toes like Sofia . She couldn't hold the knife between her toes. She just gave the chicken a quick hit. It ran around, splashing blood everywhere. They had four chickens and rice, and started cooking Somali food. The ladies from the village came, and they all had a meal together.

Afterward, Aunt Dorothy announced she had to get back to Mogadishu that night. Her plane left at ten p.m. So after that very short day together, they took her back to Mogadishu for her flight out. It was a horrible ride, bouncing in and out of huge ruts and holes on Victory Road. They always took a Somali friend along for navigator or translator, as needed. Abdi suggested they get off the rough road and go on the 'jid'—the path through the desert the trucks often took. The ground looked smoother than the broken blacktop. So they turned off onto the jid, but the ruts were too wide for their small car. They were dragging bottom and eating dust. Everyone kept telling Marc to get off the dust, but he couldn't because the ruts were so deep he was afraid they would tip the car over, and if they stopped, they would never get started again. The dust was pouring up through the floorboards. They all had scarves over their faces and were choking. By now, Aunt Dorothy was saying, "Why did I come?"

They got to Mogadishu just in time for her flight. She pleaded for time to take a shower before getting on a plane, but there was only one flight a week, so she had to make that flight. Her hair was hanging with dust, and her face was covered in it. You could only see the whites of her eyes. When she got to Nairobi, her sister Pearl took one look and exclaimed she was glad she hadn't gone! Nancy asked her mother if Aunt Dorothy had given a good report on her visit with them. Her mother never did tell Nancy what Dorothy said. Until that time, her mother thought Nancy over-dramatized things in her letters. Now she had proof she wasn't.

The desert could be a place of death for many people. God designed the desert for life, but you needed experience and knowledge to survive. There were deadly snakes. "One-step" snakes were really dangerous—if you got bitten by one, people said you would take just one step and then die. You could kill them if you hit them hard right in the middle of their back before it had a chance to bite you. They told the boys if they ever ran into a snake, they should call for one of the workers from the compound and never try to handle it themselves.

One day the boys were off riding their bikes, and they came running to Nancy. "Guess what we did?" Paul shouted.

"We killed a snake!" Marc chimed in.

"Yeah, we ran over it with our bikes!" Mike championed. "Then turned around and ran over it again, then turned and did it again!"

"We killed it!" they all cheered.

They had a pet dik-dik named Susie, the prettiest little miniature antelope. She slept behind the kerosene refrigerator at night for warmth. As Nancy came into the kitchen one afternoon, there in front of her was a huge monster, the size of the screen door, hanging top to bottom, staring in at her and hissing. It was a monitor lizard looking for the dik-dik. She screamed. It didn't move. It just hung there staring at her. The boys came tearing around the corner, wondering what was wrong. They told her not to worry, then went out the other door to get some stones to throw at it, but the monitor lizard just hung there. The stones were only bouncing off. Nancy was afraid it was going to make a hole in the "screen," which was actually just a net. Mike went outside and threw a cement block at it. Finally, it lumbered away.

The crocodiles lived down by the river. If they saw anything on the bank, they would use their tails to knock it into the water, pull it under to drown it, and then eat it. The children were told they could never go near the river. Somalia was a dangerous place to live, and the children were quite obedient.

The first time Marc went to Mogadishu and left Nancy alone, he took young Marc with him to pick up their car after getting news that it had arrived in port. They took the bus down to get it. Alone for the first time with three little ones at home, Nancy made a plan. When the sun went down and the generator went off, they'd have their feet off the floor and all be tucked under their nets in bed. Nancy knew they had electricity from six to eight p.m. and at eight o'clock, everybody had to be in bed.

She had given the kids supper, washed them, and put them in their pajamas. They had wood-framed chairs with canvas that could be taken apart so they fit into a barrel-like deck chair. She was sitting on one of those chairs, reading a bedtime story with three kids on her lap. Something kept tickling her toes. Finally, she looked down and there was a huge camel spider on her foot. She screamed and jumped, making the bookcase divider behind them fall over and crash, scaring the kids. She told them to get on their beds as quickly as they could, and told Mike to come and help her. She handed him a broom, saying they had to move fast. The lights were going off in a few minutes, and they couldn't have that spider in the house.

Mike was running around with a broom, she was running around with a dustpan, looking behind everything trying to find the poisonous spider. Just as they heard the electric motor winding down, the spider came running out from behind the fridge. There was a little crack beneath the door leading outside, and the spider flattened itself and crawled out. Mike and Nancy jammed rags and towels beneath the door and high-fived each other, then she told him to get onto his bunk. As she turned to go into her room in the dark, there were two big eyes staring at Nancy. She almost had a heart attack, but Mike grabbed the flashlight and assured her. "It's a bullfrog, Mom, don't worry." He threw it outside and then crawled under his net. She found out later, it was a bullfrog Paul had brought in.

It was just a night to never forget. By the time Marc got home, she had recovered, and was so happy to see him. She had totally lost track of what month they were in! There was no change of seasons. She had not begun to think of Christmas. But Marc came back with an aluminum Christmas tree he had found at the Italian store. He had also bought a gift for each child, reminding her it was mid-December, and that they would soon have their first Christmas in Somalia with the kids. She was thrilled.

CHAPTER 21

A String of Events

"Some stories are worth sharing as long as you understand they are events the Holy Spirit strung together."
— *Marc Erickson*

Bulo Burte, 1970

A teenager ran by and grabbed Marc's shoes when he was working on the basketball court. He chased after the boy and caught him. The boy started screaming and hollering, saying his father would kill him if he knew what he'd done, so Marc let him go. Then the boy went home and told his father that Marc had beaten him up and other outrageous stories.

The next thing Marc knew, the police arrived to arrest him, and he was taken to the police station. The policeman who addressed Marc told him he had received his training in Texas and liked America. He also told Marc he had a couple of choices in this matter. He could either have the chiefs judge him or he could have the judge give him a court date. He said he would prefer to talk to the chiefs. The policeman agreed, saying that was a good choice.

They went down to the village together. It was the biggest

thing that had happened in Bulo Burte in ten years. The doctor was on trial! When the chiefs came, they couldn't believe it. The white doctor was letting them take charge of what the penance was going to be for all the stories the boy had obviously fabricated. They all stood up, and one after another chimed in, "You're our doctor. We really like having you here. We're not going to cause trouble for you." They told him they don't spank their kids. Marc knew he hadn't spanked the kid, but that's what the boy had reported.

Someone yelled out, "A thousand shillings!" That was what they wanted to fine him so they could get the thousand shillings. Then Marc talked about how they raised kids in America, and they all talked about how they raised theirs. Finally, they conceded and said, "Can you just give us twenty shillings, Marc?" He paid the twenty shillings. But what had made the difference was how much it meant to them that he had talked to them as though they were in charge of him. After that meeting, he could do no wrong. The chiefs trusted him, and it opened up the whole town for the family. They felt safer after that.

If Marc and Nancy had known how dangerous it was in Somalia, they probably wouldn't have gone. They had no idea until they finally got there. There were the crocodiles in the river near their house. At night they would hear the water splashing. When it was extra loud, they knew the camel drivers had come. They would take their camels down into the river to wash them as they headed south to markets in Mogadishu.

Marc stayed in shape by going out for a run early every morning. Mussolini had marked off every ten kilometers along the highway with posts. So he would run eight kilometers out and eight kilometers back. Since he had been a track runner, that was easy for him, but it was hot. He lost forty pounds and looked like skin and bones, but the heat didn't bother him at that weight. The camel drivers thought it was funny to see the white doctor running. They would come along beside him, even running backwards in their flip-flops because they were so strong. Marc realized they were getting to know each other, and then there was no way they were going to cause harm. It became a good place to live, a wonderful place.

Dahir, the young man who stole vegetables so he could eat breakfast with the Ericksons, and who had been kicked out because he came to Christ, stayed in the kids' room with them.

One day he heard his father had a boil on his head, and he went home to check on him. When he saw how serious it was, he went back and told Marc about it. Marc agreed he needed help and went to see him to lance the boil. His father could have died if not treated. Because of Marc's kind care of his father's boil, Dahir's parents let him move back home and even approved of him being a Christian. They finally saw the doctor and his wife were for them and not against them. It was another God thing!

A baby was born in the hospital, and about a month later showed up with a fractured clavicle. The parents said it had happened at the hospital during delivery, and the hospital owed them money. They were getting a court date to sue Marc and the hospital. Marc went down to see the judge. Marc didn't yell at them about the obvious scam (which is what usually happened). He just asked for a court date and told them to make arrangements for a trial because he believed it was going to happen. But the day before the trial, the young father showed up at the hospital all upset with a note that said it was all a lie. Marc hadn't broken the clavicle of his child. His wife had accidentally dropped the baby. He apologized, and then he left. God intervened again.

"What had really happened was this," Marc explained. "Usually, when they said they were going to do something to the Europeans, the whole village would talk about it. It was their entertainment. But when they talked about how they were going to get all this money out of the hospital, a Colonel in the Army was sitting in the back of the room having tea. Marc had taken care of his wife earlier for an illness. And he said, 'Come here and tell me what lies you guys have cooked up this time.' So the man told him the whole story, and he said, 'That's really interesting. Do you know what you're going to do? You're going to sit down here and write a letter. I'm going to dictate it, and you're going to write it.' He wrote the apology. And that just ended the whole thing. It was a miracle. When God sends you, you're just along for the ride. I'll bet there will be a lot of people in heaven from that time we don't even know about. People gave their hearts to Christ because of what they saw happen. They saw the miracles God was doing."

Around this time, Marc was taking care of a man with a terrible wound that had an atrocious odor. Everybody had cleared out of the clinic except the nurse when a car drove up. It was the Mayor. "I told him that I could be with him in a few minutes. Well, apparently anything less than a second was too much for him, so he left. The next car that came up was a police car, and they arrested me. They put me in the car and drove me to the police station. Everybody was there. It was a show of power to intimidate me. The Mayor asked me to come into his office and shut the door. Then he said, 'I understand you're a runner.' I said, 'That's true.' And he said, 'Can I run with you?' I told him I'd love it if he would. He weighed about three hundred fifty pounds. I told him I'd see him in the morning at six o'clock. Then he dismissed me. That's how I got out of it. There was no confrontation or anything, but he never did show up to run."

Abdi Shakur came to Marc one week after he became a Christian and said his sister was in a TB hospital in Mogadishu. She was dying, and he asked Marc to go with him and treat her. They drove to the hospital, and Abdi told Marc to wait. He was going in the front door and would come out the back door to take Marc up to see his sister.

They went up to the fourth floor, and there was Abdi's sister. They got the medicine to her, and she lived. But Marc wasn't there for five minutes when he noticed secret police come in. They took him downstairs to the basement, shone a bright light in his face, and started interrogating him. Marc told them he was a doctor and had come to see Abdi Shakur's sister who had tuberculosis.

"They questioned me for about two hours. They were sure I was a CIA spy. They wondered why else I would be there? And then it struck me. What better place to hide three hundred Parliamentarians? When the Communists took over and killed the President, about three hundred people from the Parliament had disappeared. Nobody knew where they were. They hid prominent people in that hospital with the TB patients. They knew nobody would go there, and from that point on, they were sure I was CIA. They figured I knew everything they were doing and left me alone."

With the realization they couldn't stay in Somalia long-term, Marc began to send out application letters for medical mission positions in other African countries. He even volunteered to work for the Somali Government Hospital without salary. Meanwhile, their mission head assumed they were leaving the country because they were afraid. That wasn't it at all. But the man in charge of the Government Hospital told the mission head that Marc had volunteered to work for him, but the Hospital couldn't hire him, since he was sure Marc was working for the CIA. Then the missionaries finally understood. Marc's decision to leave wasn't because he was frightened, he just wanted the freedom to baptize new believers.

After that, the mission head became a close friend to Marc. "I remembered when the Communists took over Cuba, they kicked the Christians out within two years. I told the missionaries at our compound, it would be a year at the most before they'd be kicked out. They didn't believe me. But I was right. All the missionaries were out of Somalia within two months of our leaving. Then they realized what I told them was true. And to their credit, just before the missionaries left, they took all those kids we had prayed with, out into the Indian Ocean early in the morning, and baptized them all. That was pretty special."

But there was no response to Marc's other mission applications. Marc didn't know there had been a mail strike in Great Britain for four months. His letters never went anywhere; in fact, the mail had piled up in Mogadishu until it was finally bulldozed into the Indian Ocean.

Marc had moved his family to Africa with no intent of going back to the States to live. A lateral move to a place where he would be needed would be better than returning home and looking for something there. But when he didn't hear anything, they thought their only option was to go back to the States.

The last day they were in Bulo Burte, twenty-five young men Marc had played basketball with lined up to say they had decided to follow Jesus. One after another, they said, "I'm a Christian." One of the young men was the son of the Commander of the Army at the Base there, Captain Gad. He said to his son, "What's with this guy who plays basketball with you? Does he talk to you about politics? What does he talk to you about?"

And his son said, "He talks to us about Jesus."

As it ended up, Captain Gad didn't care. He protected Marc. But most of all, God had protected them. "If you are obedient, God does the rest."

Before the Ericksons left, Marc went to say goodbye to Captain Gad, who was now not only Commander of the Base, but he was also Commander of the District. The District Commissioner ran everything. All the elders were there, and all the chiefs were there when Marc gave him an Italian Bible. He responded as though he'd received a Christmas present.

"He was so excited. I really didn't know if it meant anything to him or not."

But many, many years later, Ahmed and Marc were talking, and Ahmed asked him, "Do you remember Captain Gad, Marc?"

"Sure I do."

And Ahmed said, "He still has your Italian Bible on his desk.'"

Finally, the car was packed with their suitcases and several boxes. They were ready for their last trip south on the Victory Highway to depart Somalia for the U.S. They had given away most everything in Bulo Burte, but they still needed to return the boxes of Arabic Bibles to mission headquarters in Mogadishu. It was night, and they were about five miles out of Mogadishu when they came to a roadblock. They stopped and wondered what was going on when a policeman came and shone his light on them. They were searching all the cars, and Marc and Nancy both knew if they found the Arabic Bibles, they would be in big trouble.

They were told to unload the car and get everything out. "We were terrified but praying," Nancy said. Then the policeman looked at Nan and shined the light in his own face and asked if she remembered him. It was the same policeman who had stopped her that day in Mogadishu when she took the kids to the beach instead of going to the prayer meeting. Without unloading anything, he gave orders to let them go.

"And we went on, with nothing unloaded or inspected. I hadn't understood at the time I'd met him earlier, what that had been about. Now I knew God used the earlier encounter for our departure. There were so many days like that, where we just felt, Okay God, You're here and you're in control."

The two years in Somalia had changed them all. They had moved into a sea of disease without any fear. They couldn't even speak the language. It was one hundred-ten degrees every afternoon, there were mosquitoes everywhere, malaria was everywhere, and danger was all around them. The country was in turmoil. "We had gone into a culture that was very much like Abraham's. You'd watch people come out of the desert in long robes, turbans, and flip-flops. They lived for poetry. I'm sure Abraham knew about poetry. But God was leading us back to the States. I really enjoyed being the doctor in Bulo Burte because I loved the people. And because I liked them, they liked me. In Somalia, death is always within a day's reach of everybody. You just never knew what was going to happen."

CHAPTER 22

But God: Summary of Somalia

"As for me, I believed that the only healing hope for my nation was the redemptive love of Christ, not violent conflict."
— Ahmed Haile

"God took us to the desert to meet Ahmed," Marc said, summarizing their time in Africa. "He found us. God sent him. He chose Christ and stood firm."

SIM had four mission stations in Somalia, with one couple or two single ladies at each station. Except where the hospital was, it took more staff to run a hospital. As soon as someone left for furlough from a smaller station, someone else had to move in to cover that station. They never left one person alone at a station. If the station was empty, SIM would lose the building and the investment of the station. It was always hard. You lived out of a suitcase. You couldn't put down roots and get to know the community if you had to keep moving. But that was the way they did things.

"The missionaries there before us were amazing people," Nancy said. "I felt so inadequate. I needed reminding every day that it was Christ in me that was going to make any difference, and I prayed. This work could not be done by my talents or my gifting. Even for those that had been there for a long time, all doing faithful work, it seemed easy to forget to depend on the Lord. It was easier to say, I can do this, and I can do that, OR I am better at that."

"I came to understand why some of them would get upset with me personally," Marc said. "I had been practicing bush medicine in Shashamane with all these fine doctors, with resources. When we went to Bulo Burte, the hospital was basically a midwifery center. Somalis didn't believe in surgery, and the women weren't sure they needed me. But when Joy returned from furlough and found out I was playing basketball with the young men, she said it was the answer to her prayers. Those faithful women couldn't reach the men who were the key to the culture."

"Even though those precious servants were never able to go back to Somalia, they are now working with Somalis all over the world," Nancy added. "God opened a window of time for us. We thought it would be for the rest of our lives; it turned out to be only a year and a half. The day we left, the house was full of people who came to tell us they had come to Jesus. We had no clue! It was a powerful reminder: we never know how God is working or what He is capable of doing through us. What a sendoff that was!"

Marc received a precious, humble letter from Dr. Adair years later apologizing. She said that if Marc and Nancy hadn't been so bold and moved so fast in sharing God with everyone He sent to them, they wouldn't have seen the fruit of their work in Bulo Burte. It was about taking hold of the opportunities God had given them.

They had not left Somalia because of the situation in the country. They weren't afraid of the tribal wars or the Communist takeover. It wasn't because of danger. But that door had closed. It was never in their thoughts to bring Somalis home with them. They had all they could do to bring their own family back and find out what God's next assignment was for them. He had a better plan. They knew their independent spirits were not always right, but trusted God had a place for them somewhere. "We just had no clue where."

PART THREE

Who Are You?

CHAPTER 23

Seven Moves, Seven Months. Family of Seven

"To be fully alive, fully human, and completely Awake is to be continually thrown out of the nest."
— *Pema Chödrön*

Milwaukee, Wisconsin 1971

The family arrived back in the States with one more child than they had when they left, stopping first in Boston where Marc had applied for a residency in psychiatry at the VA Hospital (which was part of Harvard Medical). But after a full day of interviews there, he returned to the car and told Nancy it wasn't the place for them. Nancy was just waiting for God to direct them. They decided to forget Boston and head back to Milwaukee. Their plans had been to be missionaries. They didn't know what to do next. They wanted a word from God.

"I was a grocery clerk. That chapter of my life had taught me a lot about people." Marc had graduated from medical school, but he always saw himself as a night stocker at Safeway. Now they were learning to step out of God's way, to listen and hear and obey God's voice. They had to learn to

139

trust God and be humble. They traveled on to Milwaukee, their point of departure a year and a half earlier.

A mother of five may have hoped to settle into a place she could call home, but Nancy had already learned what "home" meant to God, may not be what she had envisioned it to be. She had learned to travel light and to trust God. Marc took a part-time job as interim pastor at Lake Drive Baptist Church, the church they had attended when they lived in Milwaukee while Marc was in the military. They stayed with seven different families from the church over the next seven months. It may not have been the way they would have planned things, but they realized the most important part of any journey was the relationships God opened up along the way. They were waiting for God's leading. Home was wherever they were with God.

Val and Suzanne Hayworth and their three kids were one of the families that invited the Ericksons to stay with them— so the twelve of them shared life for a few months. "I was aware all seven of us were quite a burden and tried so hard to be helpful. The Hayworths were very interested in what we had experienced in Somalia," Nancy said. Val and Suzanne were professional musicians. Every night they stayed up late together to discuss what God was doing in the world.

One evening Val asked, "If you looked at a map today, where would you say the Spirit is moving?"

"I think Iran," Marc responded. A few nights later the Hayworths said they had decided to sell their house and move to Iran with their three children! Marc and Nancy were shocked, but knew God was working. They helped the

Hayworths get the house ready to sell and moved in with another family from the church. Then another and another and another. Lake Drive Baptist eventually hired a wonderful new pastor. When Marc's interim pastorate was over and he needed a job, Marc began working at County Hospital in their emergency department.

"What really happened to us throughout those seven months after we'd first returned from East Africa, was that we were getting to know more and more people all over Milwaukee," Marc said. "That was life-changing. If you don't really know people, you can think the worst of them. I had been a really narrow-minded, legalistic, critical person, but God kept knocking the walls down. When I discovered Christ had come to live in me, so many things changed. God loves people. The Holy Spirit was working on me again and I was experiencing God speaking."

They began looking for a house, and Nancy took the lead on this. They sensed that God was using them to reach college students and envisioned a home in the University district where students could go to college, live together, and have an evening Bible school. The beautiful old mansions along the streets overlooking Lake Michigan were being sold cheaply because nobody could afford the heat. Nancy was sitting at the laundromat with all the laundry to do that week and saw a copy of Homes Magazine. A house was on the cover with large white pillars for $13,500, and she thought even they could afford that. She called Marc, and together, they went to look at it. However, the foundation was crumbling, and they immediately knew it was no bargain. They kept looking. It was like Wonderland, from the Spartan cement block house in Bulo Burte to the East Side mansions of Milwaukee! They looked and looked.

A group of friends encouraged them to start a nonprofit that could back a Bible school. If they found a house large enough, it could serve as both home and school. They found a large house overlooking the Lake that had been home to a group of nuns. When word came it was for sale, they got excited. They even had an accepted offer. However, the Sisters of St. Mary's Hospital decided to keep the property, so, again, they kept looking. They even considered a house with nineteen bedrooms and thirteen baths.

Marc's mother, Delnora, came for a visit at that time. Being a very decisive woman, she thought their ideas were not practical and reminded Marc that he had five children. She spoke up for Nancy, boldly telling her son to buy a family home and stop the nonsense. Those houses would be overwhelming for Nancy. They found a family-sized house in the University district that was suitable for having large groups. It was perfect.

One evening, not long after they'd returned from East Africa, Marc was asked to speak for a college group at a friend's house. Among the students was a young medical student from China who had just become a Christian. As Marc spoke on Psalm 23, the Spirit was working. This man was deeply moved and, following the teaching, he approached Marc to ask if he would disciple him. Marc wholeheartedly agreed. There was no way for Marc to know at the time that his willingness to do so would be used by God to open a powerful connection to China in the future, or that this man would become an evangelist who would lead eighty Chinese students to Christ and start a Chinese church in Madison. "The Holy Spirit has used him powerfully," Marc said. "He was full of ideas and able to benefit from relationships that his father had with many important leaders in China. These leaders were all really good to him because of his father's connections in the import/export business. It gave him a lot of power."

Also unknown to Marc was that the new pastor from Elmbrook Church, Stuart Briscoe, happened to be sitting in the back row. "That night he told me he wanted to meet with me. I had heard a lot about him, but we'd never met." He had moved to Milwaukee from England while we were in Somalia to pastor Elmbrook Church. The only time Stuart had free was midnight on a Wednesday night right before he was to take off for Europe. Marc and Nancy went to their home, and they talked about their mission experience. Stuart invited Marc to come to Elmbrook to work with him.

"Teach an adult Sunday School class," Stuart said. They took his advice. Marc decided to teach Genesis. He managed to make it interesting enough so that four hundred people came to the Sunday School class. Stuart preached the first service in the morning to the four hundred, Marc would teach the next hour in the same auditorium, then Stuart would preach again to a new congregation at a second service.

One week, Stuart told Marc he had received an "I Wish"

card in the offering plate that read, "I wish all the services would be like the middle one because you don't sing any hymns or take an offering." Stuart and Marc had a good laugh! Stuart had an extensive international preaching ministry and traveled about one-third of the time, so he asked Marc to preach the Sundays he was away. Elmbrook was growing fast. The Holy Spirit was at work. Before Marc knew it, he was preaching to a thousand people, which was a new experience. He learned to illustrate the Word of God with stories about people he met in the emergency room. He believed the stories of what Christ was doing for people today were really important and he had a lot of stories. "Your testimony is your story about how the Holy Spirit is working in your own life to glorify Christ. What is important is what God does in and through real people. Revelation states that we overcome by the Blood of the Lamb and the testimonies of those that are not afraid to die."

~

Not long after moving into their new home, Marc began encouraging Nancy to start a women's Bible study with the neighbors. It was easy for him to suggest, but intimidating to Nancy, who had never even been to a women's Bible study. "Marc had confidence that God would use me, and I didn't. I was so nervous about it and kept using the kids as an excuse. But then my sister, Bev, came to stay with us, and I didn't have an excuse anymore. Finally, I wrote little notes to each woman on the block, inviting them to come on Wednesday afternoons to sit outside and talk about the Sermon on the Mount. Six women came. I hadn't met them before and was so pleased to meet them that day. But during the first part of the discussion, one of the ladies stood up and pointed to each of the women, saying, 'We're all Catholics. We don't belong here. Let's go.' And they all took their kids and left. I went inside and told Bev I would never do that again as long as I lived. I thought that closed the door to our neighborhood, and we may as well move."

But that night one of the women called Nancy and asked if she would come down to her house. She told Nancy her husband had left her and that he had been quite abusive. She was relieved but terrified and didn't know what to do. Nancy went over, listened to the woman's story, then asked if she could pray for the woman. She agreed, Nan prayed, and the woman came to Jesus that night. "I had the privilege of discipling her over the next months. That was the great blessing that came out of that experience. Little by little, the other five women became my close friends. They even trusted me to pray for them." It was a stumbling start, but she wanted to be used by God somehow, to learn to make Jesus relevant. They all knew she was a believer. Whether or not they wanted more was up to God.

Another thing happened shortly after they moved into the house on Shepard Avenue. Mohammad, one of the Somalis they had worked with in Bulo Burte, arrived at Chicago's O'Hare Airport and called them. He needed a sponsor in order to stay in the U.S. and would need someone to put up a bond. They went out on a limb and put up a $5,000 bond for him. He came to live with them and attended Milwaukee Area Technical College (MATC). At about the same time, the Hayworths called from Iran and asked if they would take in a young man they had met from Afghanistan. He had become a believer, and they wanted him to come to the US., so Marc and Nancy took him in, too. Then a young American engineering student going to Milwaukee School of Engineering (MSOE) came to live with them. So they had three college-age young men living on their third floor.

"It was really a nice place for them. It was like a dormitory. They shared a bathroom with our kids and were part of our family. We did everything together," Nancy said.

So just as they had done in Somalia, they opened up their home. By this time, Ahmed Haile also came to the U.S., helped by the Mennonites. He moved to Oregon to retake his senior year of high school. Eventually, he was planning to attend Goshen College in Indiana. On his way from Oregon to Indiana, he showed up at the Ericksons.

They didn't know he was coming, but he arrived on the very day Elmbrook was to ordain Marc. He went to the ordination service that night. "For the rest of his life, he'd repeat, 'I was at your ordination, Marc.' It's hard to put into words how close we became. We were brothers! Ahmed went on to graduate from Goshen and get a master's degree in peace studies from the University of Indiana."

Soon Marc and Nancy were off to Iran to visit the Hayworths. Val was teaching at a university, and Suzie played cello in the royal symphony. They were making connections but were having difficulty getting to know the families in their neighborhood. "We went shopping with them," Nancy said. "There were little kiosks up the street right on their block where you could buy fabric and beautiful art pieces being made right there in the shops, or fruits and vegetables." They intentionally went to at least one shop every day together to get to know the shopkeepers. They kept a little log of shopkeepers' names so that they could pray for them, and when Val and Susie went back to the shop, they could call them by name and ask about the needs they had shared. That was the opening to their neighborhood.

"In the Middle East, people are so hospitable. If you go into a shop, while you are looking around, you are offered tea and invited to take a seat. You sit for a bit and get to know each other, ask if they are married, if they have children, or how they got into this or that job? So many things lead to friendships. Val and Susie stayed there for eight years, until the Shah was deposed, and the revolution came. They far outpaced us in missions. Val eventually became the missions pastor at Elmbrook and had a ministry in Tajikistan just north of Iran. Tehran was the first step. But often the question is, how does one take the first step?"

CHAPTER 24

A Graduate Degree in the City

"Courage is Grace Under Pressure."
— *Ernest Hemingway*

Milwaukee, Wisconsin, 1971

Marc took the first available job at County Hospital, which really led to the city opening up to him. It was a walk-in clinic. He loved this because he could schedule shifts to be off for ministry evenings and weekends. He had every Sunday off. "It was fun. Milwaukee is a world-class city with people from all over the world. Something is always happening in the city, and I was in the middle of it."

He went from County Hospital to the Downtown Medical Health Services. The old Children's Hospital was on 18th and Wisconsin Avenue, and the plan at that time had been to move it out to the County grounds in Wauwatosa. But that would leave the inner city with no medical care. Milwaukee politicians told Children's Hospital they would need to put something in the inner city. But no one wanted to go back into the city. People were afraid. The Race riots had caused an exodus to the suburbs, again. It was at that time, one of the hospital administrators, Dr. Pearlman, approached Marc. He explained the County had just told him the Hospital needed to do something for the inner city, and they wanted to start a clinic downtown. He wanted Marc to staff it.

Marc didn't think he had the qualifications, so he inquired why they had chosen him. Dr. Pearlman explained it was because no one else would do it! The facility was on 24th and Wisconsin Avenue, a major thoroughfare in downtown Milwaukee. Marc knew the building and he also knew he could do the job along with his ministry because it would give him regular hours and weekends free. He asked if he could design the clinic to be a walk-in clinic with no appointments required and requested four technicians be there to assist. He would also need a resuscitation room in case someone had a heart attack. The hospital administration gave him everything he asked for. He had basically just created an urgent care service.

One morning he came in and was told there was a young woman there who refused to go home. She said she had hemorrhoids, but nobody had examined her. Marc said he would give her an exam and find out what was wrong. He firmly believed everybody had to be seen. He discovered she was "crowning" and about to give birth. The woman didn't even know she was pregnant.

On another day, a lady came in and said Marc was the worst doctor she'd ever seen. She told him he didn't know anything and yelled, "You're just useless. I have a headache, and you haven't done anything for me." She continued ranting, and Marc responded, "You're probably right." He gave her some medicine for her headache, and she went out the door. She came back the next day and told him nothing had helped, and she didn't know what to do.

He had examined her but realized he didn't know her story. He agreed with her. He was indeed a bad doctor because he didn't know her whole story. "How quickly we can make our own assumptions about another person when we don't know them." So they sat down together and talked about what was going on in her life. She told him her son was a teenager and had been in an auto accident. He had been unconscious for two months and was in the rehab hospital across the street. She sat with him all day long and didn't know what else to do. Marc thanked her for telling him and assured her when he was off at five o'clock, he would go with her and sit with her son, and they could pray.

He went over that afternoon, sat down with her, and they prayed. The next day, the son woke up. He walked out the door about a week later. "I'd like to think she became a Christian. You have to know a person's story, and you have to examine them to see what's wrong. Even if you've been practicing medicine for fifteen years and yet don't examine people or don't get their story, you're going to do bad medicine. It's no different in ministry work."

In the third year of the Downtown Medical Health Services (DMHS), they were seeing about forty thousand patients. Marc got to know the city well, but he also began to get in trouble. One man came in, and Marc began asking him how he was doing spiritually. He had just put on his gown, but he jumped up off the table, took his clothes in one hand, his shoes in the other, ran down the full length of the hospital corridor, and out the door in his hospital gown.

Three months later, a drug salesman who was a Christian friend of his came in to see him and shared how he had just been with a painter who was painting his office. The salesman was getting to know him, just talking to him, and started to ask him about God. The painter said the last person who talked to him about God was a doctor at the Emergency Clinic. He said he had been so unnerved he just left. But now, he was asking the salesman if he would tell him about Jesus. So Marc's friend told him about God, and the man gave his heart to Christ. "We just never know how God uses these small things in our days. But you can be assured, He is working."

Marc ended up leaving that job because he was sharing Jesus with patients, and that irritated one of the nurses. Some of the doctors who worked for him at that Clinic had gone on to start the Emergency Services at St. Mary's Hospital. They invited him to be a part of that group, so Marc moved from the DMHS to St. Mary's. There he learned about all the drugs on the Eastside and all the artists the area attracted. He discovered it was a unique part of Milwaukee. He worked at St. Mary's for twelve years and loved his time there because the Sisters of St. Mary's gave him permission to talk to people about the Lord all he wanted to. There was freedom to pray with patients about their spiritual needs, and that was what he loved. He would come home with a story a day and believed it was important for a pastor to be a part of the suffering of the city.

He would come off a twenty-four-hour shift on Saturday

and come into church with a story to tell. It was always about somebody who had walked in the door with a need, and Jesus met them there. It made everyone think about and ask questions about what they were doing and how they could be used by Jesus—whether it was in their classroom, or in their shop or office, or wherever they were. People wanted Jesus to go with them too. It made people realize the body of Christ needed every single person, not just one.

The fact that Marc worked at the hospital and was a pastor made sense to the people of Milwaukee because they also worked their jobs while doing two or three things besides. In the course of time, a few people got injured while at church, and Marc would drive them to the hospital and stitch them up. It was to his merit that they knew he was more than just a preacher.

He got to know so many people, including the police force that brought people to the hospital and all of the nursing staff. There were always people in trouble spiritually, directionally, and relationally. He had to make sure the attitude of his life was right, then he was able to talk to them about Christ authentically. And many people came to know the Lord.

During this period, Marc was doing college ministry at Elmbrook and preaching for Stuart Briscoe when he was out of town, which was about a third of the time. They had become good friends. "At a meeting one day, one of the church leaders had demanded to know how much Marc was getting paid. Stuart stood up, started walking around the room, he went all around, and then around again. Then he stopped and responded, 'Nothing!' I was a volunteer."

Marc enjoyed emergency medicine. He would work twenty-four hours, go home and sleep for ten hours, and have the rest of the week with his family and the church. He even coached his sons' teams. Even so, Nancy began to feel their boys needed more from him. Marc began taking them one at a time to stay with him overnight at the hospital. They loved those nights in his "on-call" room.

CHAPTER 25

More Alike Than We Think

"Stay open, forever, so open it hurts, and then
open up some more, until the day you die, world
without end, amen."
— *George Saunders*

Milwaukee, Wisconsin, 1975

One of the groups Marc had difficulty relating to was the Fundamentalists, because that had been his background. He remembered how far he had been from the Lord, even though he knew the fundamentals. "I was so narrow-minded when I grew up, I didn't think anyone was a Christian except for those in our little church." Now he knew there were precious Christians across all denominations—including Catholics, Lutherans, Presbyterians, and Pentecostals. Once he was asked to speak at a church on the Southside of Milwaukee, but when the host found out he didn't speak in tongues, the pastor wanted to cancel the meeting. He said nobody on the Southside was going to listen to Marc because the Mexicans and Hispanics living there were Pentecostals. When they found out he didn't speak in tongues, they wouldn't believe he qualified as a Christian.

When the time came to speak to these Pentecostal pastors, Marc told them, every Friday morning he came downtown at seven o'clock with a little group of friends to pray over the city from the top of the Hyatt Hotel. He let them know when they turned to the Southside, they prayed for them. Nobody left. Before that, they didn't think anyone was praying for them. They didn't feel they were important. Some of the people who came that evening became Marc's good friends. "The problem with the church is prejudice. The Catholics think we hate them, the Lutherans think they don't need anybody else, the Pentecostals speak in tongues and can do miracles the rest of us can't. Everyone has a reason why they don't need anyone else. But when God brought us to Milwaukee, He helped us get to know people across all the denominations, which was a really good thing to happen to me because I had been so prejudiced. I began to see I was the worst Pharisee. I was even worse than Paul. God has made each of us unique and has gifted each as he saw fit, not so we could be proud or divided. I needed God to change me."

And this is how their ministry kept growing, through the Holy Spirit. Their home on the Eastside was always open to students. They had a large Monday night Bible study for about one hundred students and a Saturday morning discipleship group. When they outgrew their home, they moved the group to the Lutheran Student Center for a Friday night outreach. They began each Friday night with supper for fifty kids at their house and then they went to the campus to invite students to the Student Center. This group eventually moved into the former J. Pelman Theatre on Oakland Avenue.

The student leaders wrote and composed music and created drama each week on current topics of discussion taking place on campus. Then Marc would wrap up the evening with a Word from Jesus to similar questions and issues of His day. God continued to speak to Marc as he studied the Word.

During the time Marc and Nancy were settling back into life in Milwaukee, and Marc into his new position at Elmbrook in Brookfield, twenty miles west of the city, Stuart was speaking to pastors all over the world. He had gone to West Africa and met with the head of SIM International. Stuart told him he had one of their missionaries on his staff. When they asked who it was, he said it was Marc Erickson. Their response was that Marc was a real troublemaker. When Stuart returned to the States, he met with Marc to get the full story. So Marc told him about their time in East Africa, and the two men decided they were kindred spirits. About a year and a half later, Stuart visited with the people Marc and Nancy had served with in Somalia. The missionaries told Stuart they wished Marc and Nancy were still there. After they had left, the missionaries realized the couple's boldness had been correct, and they also began to do things differently with renewed courage.

~

With Marc now on staff at Elmbrook, much of his schedule was taken up at Elmbrook. The children were all attending Hartford Avenue, a public grade school on Milwaukee's East Side, and had also started going to youth group at Elmbrook on the west side. The travel back and forth to the church was becoming overwhelming. At the time, Milwaukee schools had also begun bussing students out of their neighborhoods, and the prospect of their children spending an hour on the bus each day to and from school seemed too much. So Nancy found a house near Elmbrook, sold their East Side house, and put the kids in Waukesha schools. The school was out of control, and the Erickson boys hated it. "To them it seemed it was all discipline with no learning. We knew that bright kids who loved school could not survive in that environment," Nan explained.

The family agreed to pray through the summer to find a solution. They stumbled upon Brookfield Academy, a classical school of basic education. The twins took an entrance test and were admitted. The headmaster taught Hebrew, Greek, and Latin, and was a Jesuit scholar. The boys were excited to begin. Up until that time, Marc and Nancy had been big proponents of public education, but in their situation it was no longer working.

They moved the twins that year, and little by little they moved the other three. Nancy was thrilled their children once again came home each day enthusiastic about what they were learning, whether it was in literature, science, math, history, or anything. "Marc and I looked at each other and realized that neither of us had really had a good education. We felt we'd never been educated. So we began to tap into what the kids were learning. We read the great classical stories they were reading, talked about them together, and joined in their excitement." Soon they were bringing other kids home and

157

they would stay for supper, and join the great discussions around the dinner table. In this way they were able to get to know many of their kids' friends. Marc was still working at St. Mary's in addition to Elmbrook and soon began coaching the school track team. It was another good opportunity to spend time with the kids and their friends. Through coaching, Marc also got to know the parents of their children's friends, who came to respect his influence on their own children.

The University of Wisconsin-Milwaukee college students who had attended their Eastside Bible studies followed the family out to Brookfield. Monday night Bible studies continued with a packed house every week. They built an addition on to the house and doubled its size so they could fit one hundred students there.

Marc came home from the hospital one evening to find the house filled with college students. After twenty-four hours at the hospital, he was so tired he told the kids there would be no meeting that night and they should all go home. Nancy thought it rather strange. They were all just out the door and driving off as a tornado came through. It tore huge trees right out of the ground, and took the roof off the house next door to them. They had no idea it was coming. But the students all got out in time and no one was hurt. It was another illustration of God's leading and protection.

Marc was taking every opportunity he could get to preach. He worked with the Christian Business Men's Committee (CBMC), and started teaching at the Scanda House, a restaurant on Highway 100 and Oklahoma Avenue, for ProBuColls (Professional Business Collegiate). This was a Wednesday night young single adults group his friend John Fisco put together that happened to include a lot of couples. He taught there once a week. The Scanda House closed at nine p.m. but allowed them to meet there while they cleaned the floors. It was a good evangelistic outreach. They could reach people with the Word of God without being in a church. Marc continued that ministry for twelve years. John Fisco would set everything up and Marc would just show up, get a Diet Coke, and stand up to teach for sixty minutes. There was no music, no follow-up, no offerings, that was it. John did a lot of the footwork, he just wanted Marc to teach. The purpose was to teach the Word in a neutral place without getting people to leave their church and come to Elmbrook. It served a lot of church and unchurched people.

Elmbrook was growing fast and had neighborhood groups meeting throughout the city. Stuart had begun to ask some of the groups whether they were thinking of becoming a church. There were four groups on the Eastside of Milwaukee that had been meeting together. Nobody wanted to leave Elmbrook, so Elmbrook started sending some of the pastoral staff to preach on Sunday nights at the Junior Achievement Center, combining these four groups. They did that for a solid year. That's when Peter Wilkes arrived at Elmbrook. Peter was an English physicist teaching at the University of Wisconsin — Madison. He felt called to preach. Marc suggested to Stuart that if Peter wanted to take over his preaching responsibilities at Elmbrook and do the college ministry, Marc would help with the new church plant on the Eastside. So Peter was called to Elmbrook. "Peter was a wonderful friend and extremely brilliant. He was largely self-taught. When they wanted him to teach at the University in England, they had to give him an undergraduate degree so he would be qualified to teach!"

The four neighborhood groups from Elmbrook continued to meet on the Eastside, and together they were getting more and more excited about becoming a new church. They wanted Marc and Nancy to come and meet with them. This was the time of "white flight." Those that were able to move were moving to the suburbs, and the churches had followed. Marc felt called to help bring the church back into the city. "We thought if those groups would agree to move into the city, we would help them do that." In the early 70s, gas prices were skyrocketing, and the twenty miles each way was costly, but the chances of these groups breaking free from Elmbrook and moving into the city still seemed slim. They were suburbanites, there were racial tensions and related trauma in the city. There were riots, and many families were afraid. Marc didn't think it would happen, but when they were able to make arrangements to meet at Hartford Avenue School, the same school their kids had attended, Marc agreed to be their pastor.

Hartford was the first Milwaukee school that allowed a church to use its building for Sunday worship services.

CHAPTER 26

A New Brook

"Courage is what it takes to stand up and speak;
courage is also what it takes to sit down and listen."
— Winston Churchill

Milwaukee, Wisconsin, 1980

On Easter Sunday 1980, Eastbrook had its first service at Hartford Avenue School on the corner of the University of Wisconsin-Milwaukee campus at Hartford and Maryland Avenues. Since Marc had been preaching at the Scanda House and at Elmbrook, he had a large following of college students in the area, so the auditorium was full that first Sunday. Soon more people came from surrounding neighborhoods, and a new church was established.

Martha Wilson came to Milwaukee around the time Eastbrook had its launch and was looking for a church home. She was staying at the YMCA on 9th and Wisconsin Avenue and in training for retail management. While she was still at the Y, she heard about a service called Daybreak, held at the downtown Y early on Sunday mornings. Marc was preaching there, and Martha still remembers her experience. "He was talking about the Holy Spirit. I'd only heard the

161

Holy Spirit referred to at the end of prayers in my church. I was a Christian, but I didn't know about the Holy Spirit!" She knew there had to be more than just going to church. Something was missing, but she didn't know what. As she took in Marc's message, she realized. "I felt like I was sitting under a waterfall. I thought, this is what it's all about. It's about the Holy Spirit in you." It was a turning point in her life, and she started attending Eastbrook.

She was at the first Sunday service in April 1980 and noticed a big component of university students and people from the Scanda House attending that day. When Eastbrook began, it already had a critical mass of committed believers. She loved the worship and teaching but remembered standing in the hallway crying to herself one Sunday. "There was only a handful of people who were Black, like me. I felt, Lord, really? Can't we have some more of us? But I knew it was where the Lord wanted me to be because I needed the teaching that I found there and the community."

Martha had grown up in a church where there was a lot of preaching and participated in many church activities. "I was taught about personal salvation and eternal life. I was not taught about what it meant to be in the Body of Christ, and that we each have a role to play. We are each empowered by the Holy Spirit to walk in obedience and love." She looked carefully at those attending the service and saw people who were trying to align their lives with what they heard on Sunday morning. "It was a group of people not "playing church". Eastbrook wasn't about being religious. Everyone was a part of a small group, and everyone served and got to know others. It was really powerful. We weren't there just for ourselves. We were part of a larger mission and Marc was a visionary. That's what brought me to Eastbrook. It was like a breath of fresh air."

As it had been since the beginning, Marc's vision for missions was about targeting the hard places. Somalia had reopened to Eastbrook, and they were in the process of putting a team together. Martha was interested in joining the mission team, and Marc told her she should talk to Ahmed Haile to see what he had to say about Somalia. The team started getting together to pray for missions, and Ahmed was coming to those prayer meetings. There was a lot of prayer for Somalia, and that's how Ahmed and Martha got to know each other. Eastbrook designated the Horn of Africa as an unreached target area, and Martha was on the subcommittee.

Mark Hagert was the first staff person Eastbrook hired. He was single at the time and offered to do the accounting and books. Marc said they needed an office, so they found office space on Capitol and Wilson Drive. Nancy was always behind Marc as God was leading. She took the kids with her to clean the basement office space they'd rented. She bought some indoor/outdoor carpeting that was cheap and found some used desks. They had no money, so they went to Goodwill to buy furniture. They put in a phone and called it an office. There was a sweet young woman named Linda Reuter they hired as their first secretary.

The church kept growing, and in 1982, another couple

from the neighborhood, Bill and Dee Wenzler, came to Eastbrook. They volunteered to help in any way possible. Since Marc and Nancy didn't know them, they decided to have lunch. For months, they went to Turner's Hall every Tuesday. Bill would come with his yellow legal pad and ask Marc questions. He was always wanting to learn. Dee was a musician and brought many of the artists from the community with her to church. "I was terrified of artists," Marc said. "I didn't understand them at all. I needed someone to help me with the arts community on the Eastside."

Eventually, he asked Dee to join the pastoral staff and be the pastor to the artists. She was added to the staff. "She loved it; it was like Christmas for her every day! She was amazing on the piano; she just sat down and played, and I asked her to also lead worship. Bill had his own unique gifting. He was an architect by training and had his firm in the city. He was particularly well-known for church architecture. But architecture goes up and down with the economy; he had time on his hands at that time and a great heart for ministry. We put him in charge of City Ministry. We quickly realized God had brought us these two high draft choices. I didn't know why God would be wasting them on our tiny little church. They were so gifted. To this day, I don't know how we got Dee or Bill Wenzler. They were such a help. They became real pray-ers; it was like having two monks in our church."

Eastbrook quickly outgrew Hartford Avenue School, but where could they go? Bill had connections that helped get them into Riverside High School. It seemed to Marc that Bill knew every key person in the city. He knew all the teachers at Riverside, introduced Marc to the principal, and before long, the church moved to Riverside High School. It was the perfect choice for the next fifteen years. MPS didn't have a contract with them, but they continued to meet there for fifteen years, paying bare minimum rent at $1000 a month. The Wenzler's son, Ed, and his wife, Georgine, came next. Ed would set up the sound system each week. "There would have been no church if Ed hadn't made the sound system work. Ed and Georgine grew in their faith as they served."

Eastbrook was eventually told they could stay at Riverside two more years and then would have to move. Those years at Riverside had allowed them to become a strong city church, while pouring money into missions overseas. The search for another location began. The congregation was growing, and it was difficult to find a place in the city that could meet their many space needs.

Marc acknowledged that it took a very patient congregation during those years leading up to finding a facility they would eventually own. Every week, they set up church and took it down: the sound system, Sunday school classrooms, and nursery, an hour before and an hour after services. The rent agreement required them to hire one staff person from Riverside to open and close the doors and be on the premises. They hired an elevator operator. He never said much, but he would help take people up and down the floors as needed. Eventually, when they found their new church building, they wanted to thank the elevator operator for his service. He had become a part of the Eastbrook family. He acknowledged the thanks but said, "I'm coming with you."

CHAPTER 27

All God's Children

"For God so loved the world, that he gave his
only Son."
(John 3:16, NIV)

Milwaukee, mid 80s, St. Mary's Emergency Department

A terrible odor suddenly permeated the hospital one day. Marc was told there was a guy waiting to see him who was quite drunk and tried to pick up a skunk. He stank. Marc told the nurses to get the man out of the building and into the parking lot. From a distance, Marc yelled out instructions for the man to go home and wash himself in tomato juice.

The next day the man was back in the emergency room and the same smell came with him. They ushered him back out to the parking lot. Marc went out and asked him if he'd washed in the tomato juice. He said, "No, I drank it." They all had a good laugh.

Marc was learning a lot about the city again and meeting many people who needed Christ. He loved these people, like Percy Tyler, a big black man he met when he came to the emergency department for help. Marc was in one cubicle talking to a guy who was dying because of advanced stage liver disease from alcoholism. Marc told the man he had to stop drinking or he would die. Marc knew he needed the Lord and asked the man if he could pray for him. All of a sudden, Marc heard someone say, "If there's someone talking about the Lord down there, tell him to come and talk to me!" That was Percy. He told Marc that years earlier, he had been working at a steel mill when one of his friends fell into a vat of molten iron. He instinctively reached in and pulled him out, though he couldn't save his life. But Percy was burned so terribly he could never work again. The steel mill gave him a settlement and he went and bought a mink farm just when it was going out of business. He lost everything.

Marc had a little Bible study he started at the Astor Hotel every Thursday morning, and Percy started coming to that. He'd come and pray the same thing each time: "Lord, word my mouth. Thank you for letting me get up this morning. Thank you for your strength." When Percy had heart surgery and didn't have any way to get home, Marc let him use his car. The ER staff laughed and told him he'd never see that car again. It took Percy a long time to bring it back because he forgot where he'd parked it, but he brought it back.

Percy got to know Bill and Dee's younger son, John, who put together a jazz band. When John had his first jazz concert, he asked Percy if he would come and open the concert in prayer. Percy began to pray in his booming bass voice: "Lord, this is not a funeral, this is a celebration!" He went on to pray for about ten minutes. John recorded that prayer.

When Percy first became a Christian, he was fishing

in Milwaukee's Estabrook Park. Lightning struck the tree beside him, and he thought he was going to die. When he recovered from the shock and realized he was still alive, he also discovered his arthritis was healed and leaped for joy! The Erickson boys loved Percy. Paul wanted to go fishing with Percy, so Percy arranged to pick him up at five o'clock. Paul assumed he meant five p.m., but Percy came at five a.m. Paul was a high schooler then, and Percy wanted him to rent a boat and take him out to Oconomowoc Lake. They fished for hours and didn't catch a thing. Paul came home and said, "I don't know what that was all about." Nancy asked if he had a good time, and Paul said, "Oh, yeah. I like being with Percy!" Paul learned that life is more about relationships than catching fish.

Percy was a window into the Black community for Eastbrook, and that was very special. When he died a few years later, Marc was asked to speak at his service. John brought the recording he had made of Percy praying at his concert, but Marc didn't know that. The funeral home was packed full of friends and family when the undertaker came out and welcomed everyone. People got up to talk about Percy, saying how crazy he was and how they all knew he was a fool. Marc listened as they had nothing good to say about him. He was supposed to preach a sermon and wasn't sure how to respond as he stood up. That's when John put on the recording of Percy saying, "This ain't no funeral, this is a celebration!" Everyone heard Percy's voice and thought he had come back to life! People started screaming, "He's alive, he's alive! Oh no!" Nancy was sitting between her two terrified little girls. Three or four people went up to Marc and held onto him because they were so scared.

Percy was laid out in an extra-long coffin because he was 6'6". When everybody heard his voice, they really believed he had come back to life. They had no idea it was a recording; it never occurred to them. The girls were holding on to Nancy, saying, "Mom, Mom, where's Percy?" She didn't know what was going on either. John didn't let anyone know that it was a tape. Then Marc preached the Good News of Christ's forgiveness for sinners, and many were prepared to listen.

"And so we buried him," Marc said. "Percy came from another culture altogether, but he was transformed by Jesus Christ. He was our brother, and his death gave us a chance to share the Gospel with so many we would not have met otherwise.

~

Marc's preparation for ministry was in medicine. There were a lot of people who needed to have a doctor understand them more than they needed someone with seminary theology. Eastbrook was a refuge. "We had a number of schizophrenics attending, and we found a way for them to come and participate in the service. I told them to simplify their lives as much as they could, show up for worship, and have a few friends they trusted. When they did that, actually, there was a lot of healing."

Some people were difficult at first, but when God got ahold

of them, they changed. Before long, Marc couldn't remember what the people were like when they first came. One man who started attending said he was there looking for babes. He was bipolar. As long as that was his motivation, Marc had to tell him he couldn't come. "He couldn't take advantage of the young women at Eastbrook. He would destroy people. It was hard, but I told him I would physically throw him out if I had to." Two years later, that man showed up again. This time, he let Marc know he had Lou Gehrig's disease and didn't have very long to live. "The man was repentant and realized he needed Jesus, so we prayed together."

The last three months of his life, that man was transformed. At his funeral, people wanted to know why so many had shown up for the service. He hadn't been at Eastbrook for very long. "When I gave the message, I said they were going to see Larry again because he was in heaven." People gasped. Some had only come to make sure he was dead because he had done so much harm. Following that, Marc received angry letters for several years saying that man couldn't possibly be in heaven. But Marc knew that man's life had been proof of Christ's ability to transform a life.

Marc had learned in ministry that you found out the truth about many people you wished you didn't know. If you are not a believer, you can choose your friends; he could not. It was his job to love everyone that God sent. Eastbrook had an abnormal number of difficult people in the early years. "But everyone who hung in there grew. We had to accept the people God sent and offer hope." It was the reason he and Nancy loved Eastbrook. People were fitting together into the most beautiful mosaic they had ever seen. Every once in a while, they would hear people say it was more than they could deal with. Seeing the extremes of opinions and different backgrounds of people could make some feel almost polluted. But they believed strongly that it was God's work, and the unity in diversity was beautiful.

Another issue they experienced was that people were afraid of mental illness and often reacted as if it were contagious. There was a group home with people wrestling with different illnesses just north of the church. A group would come to church on Saturday nights on their way back from Pick 'n Save food store with their canned goods. They would sit in the front row and pass the cans back and forth, sharing. Even though they couldn't understand much of the service, they were accepted. One woman was nonverbal. She would sit in the front row with the others, staring blankly. One day, Marc prayed with her, and when she came back, she was a different person. She said, "It's Jesus, it's Jesus!" She would come Saturday night and again for Sunday morning service and would dance when the music began. People would tell Marc that he had to get rid of her, but he wouldn't let anyone touch her. "She had found Christ, and now she was so happy that she danced. It was the only way she could express her joy."

A wonderful evangelist was invited to come one weekend from Wheaton College. Marc was able to introduce him to the woman. Marc told him he would know that the Holy Spirit was present if she started to dance. He didn't respond as though he believed Marc, but the next morning, when the congregation began to sing for worship, the woman got up and began to dance. The guest speaker was really touched. Of all the things he saw and heard about during his visit, it was that young woman that changed his life. "The girl who could only say about two words—It's Jesus."

CHAPTER 28

God's Bigger Picture

*"He is no fool that gives what he cannot keep to gain
what he cannot lose."*
—Jim Elliot

Milwaukee to Mogadishu 1981

The Vice President of Somalia sent Marc a letter asking him to come back to Somalia to rebuild the hospital in Bulo Burte. Marc flew to Nairobi to meet with the old SIM team to see who he could recruit to return with him. SIM checked it out and said they thought it was too dangerous. They had lost too much when they were forced to leave. Marc came home disappointed. However, with the written invitation from the Vice President, Marc felt Eastbrook had to take it seriously. The Church was just one year old. He presented the opportunity to the Council hoping to send someone in. They voted it down. Marc said, then he would resign from his new position as pastor and go himself. The Council held another vote. This time they were willing.

Ahmed Haile, Marc, Nancy, and two other couples flew into Mogadishu and signed a contract directly between the Government of Somalia and Eastbrook Church. The idea was to go back in and try to rebuild what SIM had left, and do primary healthcare on a developmental basis. They needed support from the government to sign the agreement. Ahmed introduced Marc to Anab (not her real name), a high-level government official in Somalia who spoke all over the world representing her government. A door back into the country began to open, and Eastbrook began to pray for a team. Marc asked Ahmed to be the leader of the team. Other missions didn't yet trust nationals in the role of leader. But Marc was adamant.

A team began to form. Martha Wilson was one of the volunteers. At that point, Ahmed and Martha were seeing each other. She went to talk to Dave Brown, Nancy's brother, and Marc's colleague on staff, to let him know. She wanted to go to Somalia, but wasn't sure she didn't have ulterior motives. He told her that most of the time we all have ulterior motives, it's good to know that, realize it, and proceed accordingly. Be wise. So Martha joined the team being formed, and plans began to take shape. Much prayer and preparation began in earnest. Bonnie and Tim Tesch, Lance and Julie Parve, Eric and Laura Gottinger, Paul and Sue Marino, Martha Wilson, Becky Boggs, Mary Pomrening, and Marc and Nancy's son, Paul, made up the first team. They had both medical and engineering gifts on the team. Bill Wenzler came out to help redesign and create appropriate housing for everyone. They also rented a house in Mogadishu for a headquarters. The team stayed in Mogadishu initially to study language, then they moved up to Bulo Burte.

Martha went as the administrative assistant and was shocked when they landed on the tarmac. She got out of the plane and wondered where the bus was that was supposed to take them to the terminal. There was no bus. The tarmac was black, it was well over a hundred degrees, the heat was laminating off the pavement of the landing strip. They were instructed to pick up their bags and carry them into the concrete building. There was a balcony with railings where people could watch the incoming passengers above her. There was no conveyor belt. She threw her suitcase on the long, wide concrete slab where airport workers pushed it along down the table. Everything had to go through the approval process. Ahmed was up on the balcony shouting down, "Martha, Martha!" He was there to get her through. She had arrived in January, wearing heavy sweaters, and she suddenly realized it was really hot. "I was cookin'!" she exclaimed, her hand becoming a fan at the memory. Ahmed got her through. Everything was about who you knew and Ahmed was invaluable. He smoothed the way for Martha and for the whole team. Ahmed opened a lot of doors others couldn't have. "I think he was God's man for that time."

Before that, Martha had only been to Canada. Here she was driving through Mogadishu, a major city, with herds of goats sharing the highway. "It was like an alternative universe," Martha laughed. Ahmed had set up a house for the team in Mogadishu (Mog) with rooms to accommodate families coming down from Bulo Burte to buy groceries and stay for a weekend. He made a place for the team to learn the Somali language. He took everyone to the Tea Shop, introduced them as the Eastbrook group and they got to know people. In order to prepare for the team's arrival in Bulo Burte, Ahmed sent Paul Erickson up country ahead of them to dig latrines and make bricks alongside the Somalis who were rebuilding the hospital and homes. When the team finally arrived, there was a compound of homes where they all lived close to the hospital.

"It was a different era, there was an openness to Christianity that is not there anymore," Martha said. "Today, there's a hopelessness, a despair. Some people say the church is the only thing that can bring hope to Somalia because only God empowers you to forgive as you've been forgiven. If you can learn to forgive, you can move forward. But if you're always in a revenge cycle, there's no end, you just keep going deeper into despair. Somalis are all Muslims, but they are killing each other for power. One clan wants power; they don't want the other to have any. The Islamic Extremists are trying to make it into a different country."

All the while the team was there, Ahmed networked with the government officials. The official most pivotal to the Eastbrook Development Project was the woman named Anab. Ahmed introduced Anab to Marc and the two would sit together for long hours to discuss faith. Eventually, she gave her heart to Jesus. When Anab needed ear surgery, she made plans to go to Germany. But Ahmed and Marc convinced her to go to America instead, where she could have the surgery in Milwaukee, be familiar with the language, and meet with the staff at Eastbrook to further support the Somali project. Anab agreed to go. Marc arranged the surgery with an ear specialist and Nancy invited her to stay with them as she recovered.

It was Anab's first time in the U.S. and she received a warm welcome from the Ericksons and members of the Eastbrook family. "I began meeting with individuals and asking questions. I could see they were different and wondered about the power I saw. I came to understand they were showing me the love of Jesus in them."

Anab wanted to work on her English, and sixteen-year-old Lisa Erickson quickly volunteered to help. In a quiet corner of the living room, Lisa and Anab would sit together hour after hour. Lisa used a simple translation of the Bible for their reading and would carefully correct any mispronounced words, going back over them again and again. "She was a natural-born teacher." Anab wanted to start with the Book of Genesis and read through to the end, but Lisa wanted her to start in the Gospel of John. Anab thought you should start a book at the beginning, so they started with Genesis. After every paragraph, Lisa would ask if she understood. They repeated this every day until they were through the Book of Daniel. Then all of a sudden, Anab said, "We can skip to the New Testament now." So they did.

The Ericksons' cars were always old and rusted out; the school their children attended was embarrassed by their cars and told the kids not to park in their lot. At one point, the boys left the car door open and backed out of the garage. They bent it back but sprung the hinge on the door so it wouldn't stay closed. It was finally permanently shut and the door unusable. It was just a two-door car, but Anab was never too proud to crawl in through the window, then off they would go.

As the months passed, Anab was told by her doctor that the flight back to Somalia would hurt her ears. Spring turned to summer, and one evening the kids had all gone to bed while Nancy was up getting ready for a family camping trip. Around midnight, Anab came to her. After all her study of the Bible and the many discussions she had had with Marc and Nancy, she had surrendered her heart to Jesus, but she carried great fear of being exposed in her Muslim country. Anab had witnessed Ahmed's arrests many times and seen him held for days on many occasions. She held high rank in the Somali government, was very well-known, and she knew it was extremely dangerous to be identified with the Christian faith. She could be kicked out of government and put in prison, but of greater concern was being put out of her own family. They sat at the kitchen table in the early morning hours, having a deep discussion. Although Anab had heard it said not to hide her faith, she told Nancy she wanted to keep it personal. She didn't want to lose her family. "Please don't tell anyone," she said, confiding the feelings that kept her awake at night. So they prayed together.

Nancy and Marc honored Anab's request. When Anab returned to her country, people may have witnessed her praying and fasting, but her decision to follow Jesus was never publicly revealed in Somalia. "We never knew what God was up to," Nancy said. "The important thing was to make ourselves available to Him day by day." The experience was life-changing for everyone, and Anab went on to become an executive in World Vision International. Her English was perfect. Before long, Paul Erickson was heading off to Somalia to live with Anab and her family.

"God uses certain things in our lives for His own purpose," Anab said about that first visit to America. "He used my ears to get my attention. He said to me, 'Sit here, I want you to learn who I am.' Imagine that. It was His calling to me. He brought me all the way from Somalia to Eastbrook so I could hear His voice better!"

~

Six months later, Marc and Nancy went to visit the team, and some Somalis welcomed them like royalty. That made it clear to them that the Somalis loved the team Eastbrook had sent. One of the top judges of Somalia invited them to a huge feast at a beautiful restaurant overlooking the Indian Ocean. The judge treated them as though they were his best friends. He had spared no expense to thank them for their return to the village of Bulo Burte; he risked his life to befriend the Eastbrook team.

Within the village, there was an important young government official who had a big house and money for anything he wanted to buy. He frightened some people living there because of his status and power. A beautiful young Somali nurse who had become a Christian caught his attention. The young man came to her father, who was just as poor as a church mouse, and told him he wanted to marry his daughter. She had little choice and married him.

One day, her husband was transferred to another part

of the country. He knocked on Marc's door and said he wanted to talk to him. Ahmed Haile was there at the time, which was good because he could translate. The man came in and sat down with them. "I won't see you again because I've been transferred, but I want to thank you for taking that little tumor off my back," the man said. This gave Marc the opportunity to tell the man he had been wanting to talk to him for years. He asked if it would be alright if he shared something really important with him. The man agreed.

"He could be an intimidating man, but he just sat there. In Somalia, you never show your emotions with your face because if you do, you lose power, so we just sat there. I gave Ahmed a heads up that I wanted to tell the man about Christ. I knew it could be our death sentence, but I needed Ahmed to help me. So he translated for me, and I shared the Gospel with this official. I couldn't tell what he was thinking. He just said goodbye, got in his car, and drove off. I thought the next person we were going to see would be the police. But the next person we saw was a messenger with the following message: Marc, thank you for telling me about Jesus. I have wanted to know about Him all my life, but no one has ever shared Him with me. I can read Italian; can you get me an Italian Bible? People in the village had made him out to be the great enemy, but it turned out he really wanted to know about Jesus. I've never forgotten that. You just can't prejudge people; you never know who God has prepared."

CHAPTER 29

The China Connection

"The Lord is my shepherd; I shall not want.
He makes me lie down in green pastures.
He leads me beside still waters.
He restores my soul.
He leads me in paths of righteousness
For his name's sake."
(Psalm 23:1-3, NIV)

In 1989, a spiritual sister from China came to the University of Illinois as a visiting scholar. She had become a Christian back in China prior to coming to the U.S. While studying at the University, this woman realized there might be unwanted attention from her from other Chinese associates on campus due to her newly found Christian faith. She called a friend to ask for advice. That friend happened to be Marc's friend, the medical student Marc discipled following the family's return from East Africa. He called Marc to see if this Chinese sister could come to Milwaukee and live with the Ericksons. Marc conferred with Nancy, and they agreed it was not the time to take this Chinese sister; there were already twelve people living in their house. However, their daughter Lisa had just graduated from Wheaton and moved back home.

She overheard the conversation. After Nancy left for the grocery store, Lisa convinced Marc she could make room for one more, and that she believed God wanted them to say yes to this woman. By the time Nancy returned with groceries, Lisa had rearranged things, called Elmbrook to enroll this Chinese woman in classes to keep her visa, and left for the train to pick her up.

Nancy was skeptical of the wisdom of that decision. But this woman turned out to be an angel of God, who helped Nancy make the whole house work that semester. "This Chinese sister was my shadow. We worked together at home and in ministry, and we loved every minute of it. She later opened up China for Lisa."

Meanwhile, Marc's Chinese friend was now working at Wheaton College and wanted Marc and Nancy to meet his family in Hong Kong. So in May 1990, they flew together with their daughter Lisa and stayed with his mother, who had recently given her life to Christ. But when they arrived, they discovered that his mother still had her Buddhist gods, which were very costly. He turned to Marc to ask him to tell her she had to get rid of them. They didn't look like any Hindu gods they had ever seen, but were big, beautiful art pieces, each worth about $10,000. They all talked and talked, and she finally said, "Can't these be sold and the money given to the poor...? Or couldn't I just give them to a friend?" Her son was quick to respond, "Would you want to give evil to a friend?" So together they went ahead and smashed them to smithereens with hammers. It was quite a lesson.

The high point of the trip was connecting with thirty

house church leaders who were meeting together one day during Chinese New Year. The visit was rather clandestine because it was risky for all thirty leaders to be together in one place. At this point, Beijing was filled with identical-looking apartment buildings, twenty stories high, and the problem was finding the right building. "Our friend told us to wait in a little park while he and his friend went ahead to find the right building," Nancy said. "Marc, Lisa, and I waited there for a couple of hours for the two men to return. We didn't speak Chinese. We didn't have any money, and we didn't know where we were or where we were going. We knew people were waiting for us, but we couldn't get to them. Eventually, our friend came back and led us to the right apartment."

One of the first people they met there was a cardiologist. She was the doctor for the Chinese church leaders. When these men became pastors, they were no longer able to be a part of the government health system. This cardiologist knew them all, and they trusted her. Marc asked her how she had found Christ, and she told them this story:

"One day, a neighbor lady came to my apartment, knocked on the door, and said, 'I've just made a great discovery about Jesus. I'd like to tell you.' I told her to stop right there and never come near my apartment or mention that name to me again. I informed her that I was a member of the Communist party and would be required to turn her in. So the lady went away. But a few weeks later, I had a massive heart attack. They took me to the hospital and tried to save my life, but I died. They took my body down to the morgue in the basement of the hospital. My husband was called and required to come to identify my body. As he was looking at my dead body, he realized I had begun breathing. So they rushed me back up to the hospital, where I woke up. I told them I knew I had died. I was in this dark place, but there was a little light up in the corner. I asked, 'Who are you?' And the light said, 'I am the God of your neighbor.' That's all. So when I got out of the hospital, I went right to my neighbor who had talked to me about Christ. I pounded on her door and said, 'Tell me about Jesus!' I saw God. And He told me that God is who you said He was!"

Sitting on a bed in that dark apartment, Marc, Nancy, and Lisa listened to the stories of these "dear saints." They had all been in prison for their faith for fifteen or more years. One by one, each of the leaders told their story. The prisons in China didn't provide food for prisoners, so family members had to bring food to them. One man wasn't married and had no family. There was a single lady in the church that brought food to him faithfully every day for seventeen years. When he finally got out of prison, they asked him what he was going to do. He said he would pick up where he'd left off the best he could. But the church asked him to marry the lady that had cared for him all those years. She had served him faithfully and had given up her own chance to get married in order to keep him alive. So they were married. "She was one of the treasures we met that day," Nancy said. "They knew what love was."

Another Christian woman spent many years in prison. When she was finally released, her husband had died. He had left her some shares of Occidental Petroleum Stock. She found out that that stock was now worth a half million dollars. She took all the money and used it to educate children of the other pastors she had been imprisoned with. "What we saw was a group of people with nothing. They all had college degrees, but no standing in society. But they had experienced the Holy Spirit and they stood together evangelizing China."

One elderly pastor explained that his job in prison was cleaning toilets. He would clean and then bow before the "throne" and talk to God. These Chinese Christians considered it a privilege to face persecution for the Name of Jesus. When oppressed, they continued on, obedient to their call, having already counted the cost. "They knew that knowing Christ was worthy of any cost! The Western church today doesn't know anything about suffering or endurance. We need to be prepared to survive suffering for His Name. We need to learn to pray, memorize the Word, deny ourselves, and know He is worthy of any price. We were undone by their faith, by Christ's Presence with them through the years, and how they obeyed God. It was like we'd been to heaven and back."

At the end of their trip, their friend took them to see his father, who Marc had met some years earlier. He was living in a penthouse, making bets from his living room window overlooking Hong Kong's horse racetrack. It was a most prestigious place. He was not interested in faith because he had no felt needs, but now he had had a stroke. Marc asked him where God was in his life. He said he didn't need God, that he was his own God. He had no faith at all. Marc told him he was going to pray that God would give him the gift of faith. Then they went back to the hotel to pack and head to the airport.

After the bags were all checked and they were ready to board the plane, a storm suddenly blew in. Their plane never came, and they were instructed to take their bags back. It was a major storm, and finally, all flights were canceled. Their friend suggested they return to his father's apartment. When they arrived, his father was sitting alone in his bedroom. Marc said, "Let's just have a little worship service in the living room." Pretty soon, they all heard, thump-thump, thump-thump. It was his father coming down the hallway with his cane. He walked into the living room and sat down as Marc was talking through the story of the Prodigal Son. His father started to cry. Marc asked if he had said something to offend him. "No, no," he wiped his eyes. "This son wants to return to the Father," and then he cried some more. This friend's father received the love and forgiveness of his heavenly Father that day. That was an example of how God was working in China. People heard the Good News and trusted Jesus for salvation.

"Then we understood why our flight had been canceled and why we had to return to his father's home. God sent the storm to welcome this father home to Him."

It was in light of the people of China that Marc had wanted to become a Christian. He was only thirteen when a missionary from China came to speak at his church. The missionary, Mr. Garrison, had lost his wife as they fled over the mountains of China on their way out of the country during the Communist takeover. When Mr. Garrison had finished speaking, he gave a call for future missionaries that would continue on with his work. Marc went forward. It was the Communist takeover that determined Marc's decision to be a Christian missionary. "I can remember that just as sure as I'm sitting here. It turned out to be a huge decision."

This trip to China was especially strategic for their daughter, Lisa. She and her fiancé, Adam Shidler, were preparing for a life of mission service. They had both studied in Israel during college and thought perhaps they would go to the Middle East. But during this trip, God called Lisa to China. Their focus began to take shape in a new direction.

CHAPTER 30

Love's Fruit

"How great is the love the Father has lavished on us,
that we should be called children of God! And that is
what we are!"
(1 John 3:1, NIV)

After their marriage in 1990, Lisa and Adam spent two years in Milwaukee preparing for missions in China. Lisa pursued a master's degree in linguistics from the University of Wisconsin-Milwaukee, while they both began building relationships with the Chinese students here. They became part of an international student outreach through Eastbrook. This group met every Friday night at Helen and David Morberg's house. David was a professor living near UWM. Since this was right after the 1989 Tiananmen Square massacre in China, George Bush issued an amnesty to let all the Chinese students stay in the U.S. that year. Most Chinese students in the States watched the media coverage with horror at what their government had done to their University colleagues in Beijing. Many became disillusioned with communism and were seeking answers and truth. Quite a few students became believers that year and began studying the Bible in earnest. It was a very unique time to be working with Chinese. Eastbrook's international outreach was a key ministry at that time. At the same time, Adam and Lisa began to teach English as a Second Language to university students at the Eastbrook Center. This ministry in partnership with the Friday night student ministry really helped many students get connected to lifelong friends at Eastbrook and continues to be a blessing forty years later.

By August of 1992, Lisa and Adam were ready to move on and had an amazing send-off picnic with about one hundred Chinese friends and church members to wish them well. Through these precious Chinese friends, they knew they would have friends waiting for them when they got to Asia. That night, Marc decided to give Lisa and Adam one more protective vaccine. This shot was recommended by the State Department for travel to China, but they ran out of time to do it, so Marc said he would get it and give it to them to save time. However, that shot caused an intense allergic reaction for Lisa. An ambulance was called, and cars were moved out of the driveway while Lisa lay motionless on the floor. Fortunately, Heidi was home and had extra epi pens because of a reaction she had had of her own to a recent bee sting. Marc gave Lisa three epinephrine shots but couldn't bring her around. Time stood still. She was rushed unconscious by ambulance to the hospital.

After a week in the hospital, Lisa came home but had a second reaction. It ended up delaying their departure for a month. At the end of September, Lisa and Adam finally flew to far Northeast China, where their friend had connected them to jobs teaching English at a Medical College. They taught in Northeast China for two years and then were able to move West and teach English with her dear Chinese sister for a number of years.

In 1994, Western newspapers were filled with stories about the "Dying Rooms of China". This referred to the government orphanages. Because of the one-child policy, babies were abandoned if they weren't "perfect" or not a boy. These abandoned babies were taken to overcrowded orphanages where many didn't survive. Lisa visited one such orphanage with a friend, and it broke her heart to see the conditions. Babies were lying in cribs with watered-down bottles of milk just inches out of their reach, not making a sound, and with no one to help. These little ones had already lost hope.

Lisa begged her Christian Chinese friends to foster some of these babies. Part of communism in China was that everyone had to work, including mothers. They were assigned jobs, and the children could stay with grandparents or be put in state daycare. No one was available, and the elderly who were watching their grandchildren didn't want to watch someone else's children too. There was a stigma against orphans that they brought bad luck. These babies haunted Lisa at night. She finally went back to the orphanage with a group of student volunteers and asked if she could help by fostering one baby. When the head of the orphanage agreed, Lisa and the Christian volunteers prayed and then picked one skinny little baby. In the assigned university housing for teachers where they lived, they had been told by the police that they weren't allowed to have anyone living with them for security measures.

Lisa had checked with her Chinese sister beforehand about bringing a baby home. She had been told to keep it a secret—a don't ask, don't tell policy—or they could get in trouble with the school officials. So, she asked one of the students to carry this baby through the gate to her house past their yard guard in a rice bag. They named this little treasure Amanda, and soon Lisa and Adam started the long process of international adoption. This turned out to be just the first child they took out of the State Orphanage. Three months after Amanda, there was a second child, Nathan, a little boy with both feet amputated. When Lisa called and told Marc of the need, he shared it with the church. The Chevako's, an amazing family from Eastbrook, came forward. It took a lot of work and about nine months to complete this adoption. During the months, Amanda and Nathan became close "siblings".

Before long, Lisa and Adam started a Bible study with high school and college-age students in their home. They were studying the Experiencing God books by Blackaby. The students grew to love Amanda and Nathan and were excited about what God could do. So they went and found an apartment for rent and asked if Lisa and Adam would help them fund it so they could take care of more orphans. The head of the state orphanage was very difficult to work with, but he agreed to their fostering more kids. Besides the student volunteers, staff had to be hired and trained, doctors had to be found, and laws had to be carefully followed for international adoptions to take place. When the orphanage leaders saw how well the children did in their care, the head of the orphanage agreed to give them more and more children. This meant they kept needing to move to larger facilities. Their Chinese sister gave this home a name which translated, meaning, the Home of Eternal Love. This Christian orphanage gradually grew and developed, and the number of children increased. As the needs increased, God brought more Chinese believers to staff it. Eventually, believers from all over the city got connected to each other through the children, and the house churches were able to know and encourage one another. Over the next ten years, they cared for sixty children.

The summers are typically warm and humid in Central China, but winters can be very cold and wet with occasional snow. Nancy arrived alone for a visit during a particularly cold spell that changed into frost and snow. She accompanied Lisa to the hospital because they had a little girl with hydrocephalus that needed surgery. The top neurosurgeon in the city arranged for them to do the surgery at a small clinic he operated in order to save them money. The small clinic was rudimentary, but sufficient. They checked out the operating room before signing off and had to send the child, a caregiver, and everything they needed with them to the hospital. "We had to go out and buy sheets and a potty, a little cook stove, food, and water thermos. The operating room was simple, but clean. Patients' beds were crowded everywhere."

Lisa was afraid of trusting this little girl for brain surgery, but the doctor assured her he had done it before and that it wasn't that difficult. He told her he was going to put a shunt into the girl's brain, down through her throat, and into her stomach. There was a medical device wholesale market nearby, and he sent them there to buy their own shunt to save money. He was doing his best to keep the costs as low as he could. "We didn't know what size or what exact kind he needed. Who would sell a shunt?" Nancy said. "But we showed the doctor's note and found a shunt in the medical apparatus market near the hospital. We took the shunt back to the doctor. A couple of days later, they did the surgery, and it was successful."

The orphanage continued to grow, and Lisa discovered a set of apartments around a courtyard that would be perfect for the children to play safely. "It was so cold. We painted and worked fast to get it ready. Lisa bought twenty-two cribs and equipment she would need." The rooms were in a square, all around a central courtyard. There was no central heat, only space heaters to warm it, which made it cold during the winter months, so she needed to find carpeting to warm it. Lisa reached out to an American man who had volunteered at the orphanage and worked at a hotel in town to see if they had any used carpeting they could donate. He told her there were garages full and could donate whatever she needed, but she would have to come and pick it out.

"When we arrived, he opened these huge commercial garages filled with rolls and rolls of used carpeting. We had to lay them out to find which were usable. There we were, standing on top of these huge piles of rolls, throwing them down, unrolling them to find what was usable, creating good piles and bad piles." The young man found a truck and delivered the good rolls to the orphanage. It was snowing, raining, and sleeting, so with frozen hands, Lisa and Nancy set to work, measuring and cutting the carpeting with box cutters to fit the carpeting into the spaces. "It warmed up the rooms. We cleaned as best we could, put the equipment in, and moved the children in, all in a very short amount of time. It would be hard to find two crazier women." It was a lot of work.

In the months that followed, Nancy put a call out to the Eastbrook Women's Ministry for used baby clothes, blankets, or toys. They collected seven hundred pounds of things. Nancy and Marc returned to China accompanied by their daughter Heidi, her husband Dan, and their baby. It was quite a sight as they passed through Chinese Customs. Heads turned, and eyes rolled at the American couple who needed all that baggage for one baby.

To raise funds for the orphanage, Lisa sent peasant art paintings rolled up for Nancy to frame and sell. "I'd take them to frame shops and then travel around to fairs and festivals. I eventually bought the materials and matted and framed them myself. It wasn't easy finding places to sell the paintings. I called all around trying to find churches and county fairs where we could show them." She eventually sold hundreds of paintings along with handmade Christmas stockings and cloth dolls with little padded jackets like the traditional Chinese baby clothes that children wore in China, all made by Lisa's Christian friends. In the end, they sent some models to a toy factory, and they made a container full of cloth dolls for them to sell. Whatever money they raised was all sent to The Home of Eternal Love.

In all, the orphanage took in those sixty children with various disabilities. They hired local Christian ladies to help and notified Eastbrook of the need for adoptive families. Ten children were adopted by Eastbrook families. Some children were adopted by families in Europe or China. The "one child" policy was the main reason many children were abandoned. Lisa always had to respect the laws and work with the China Center for Adoption Affairs in Beijing. Eventually, all but six children were adopted, and those six are still living in China— four are in care facilities, and two are on their own. As they cared for more kids, their network of house churches grew, and it changed people's mindset about orphans. Eventually, they had twenty foster homes around the city caring for children, and those families were changed. They loved the kids, and people came to see that orphans were worth loving and investing in. Some families even ended up adopting their foster children.

"This was all God's plan," Nancy said. "He had a plan all along to build his church, and it ended up that caring for orphans was a key to building that church. So, not only did the church help the orphanage, but the orphanage built up the church. It had ripple effects. We only have to be available to God. The local Chinese Church became a vital part of that ministry. And Amanda became our treasure."

What Marc and Nancy have personally seen God do in China over the last twenty years would have been enough for one lifetime. "They tell us this is the time of the Spirit in China," Nancy reflected. "The Spirit is working especially through humble servants to orphans and widows, to prisoners' families. The door for Americans to work in China opened for a while, but it's closed again. The seventeen years our daughter and her husband spent in China were strategic. God kept the right thread on hand and ready to use at the right time. He was weaving everything together."

CHAPTER 31

A Watershed

"Therefore, confess your sins to each other
So that you may be healed."
(James 5:16, NIV)

Milwaukee, mid 1990s

Up until the late 1980s and early 90s, Eastbrook was made up primarily of suburban people that grew out of the original small groups that had come from Elmbrook. The purpose of the church was to connect with the city, but it didn't happen all at once. This took time. From the beginning, they were connected to China, Somalia, and Egypt, but they still remained committed to the vision of being a church in the city. It wasn't either/or; it was both.

Relationships took time, trust had to be built, respect was earned through love and being consistently present in people's lives. Sometimes you saw changes for the better. Other times, not. People came and confessed their faith in Jesus but were also struggling with addictions. After years of love and discipleship invested in them, they disappeared. "Then we would cry out to the Lord in prayer, asking where we had fallen short?" Fifteen years passed after one such disappointment, but then, one day, I heard a familiar voice in the auditorium, received a hug, and saw what God had done in that person's life! What a day of rejoicing that was," Nancy said.

During this period, there was an Alderman in the city named Michael McGee who was passionate about the need to change the racial culture of the city. He had a call-in radio talk show on Sunday nights that was purposely inflammatory. He publicly said that he would burn the city down if there wasn't a change and rebuked Milwaukee for being the most segregated city in the nation. He was right. One of the members of Eastbrook called in to his radio show because Michael had made a comment that none of the pastors in the city had ever called him to discuss the situation. He was angry about that. This Eastbrook member proposed that his pastor would call him. Then he told Marc.

Marc made a date to go to the commando house where Michael's office was to meet with the Alderman. The commandos, a part of Father Groppi's movement, were activists determined to bring change or take down the city government. Marc's pastor friends warned him not to go because of how dangerous they had heard he was. But Marc went.

When he arrived, there were police cars in front of the commando house writing down all the license plates of the people that came to see Michael because they were threatened by him. He was considered by many to be the most dangerous man in the city. A few of the commandos let

Marc in and then went upstairs to get Michael. Meanwhile, Marc sat down surrounded by all the political propaganda around him, pastors supporting communism and Cuba. The commandos returned and told Marc that Michael wouldn't come down unless he agreed to sit out on the porch with him so everyone could see him. They sat on the porch and Michael asked Marc if he'd ever read the Book of Revelation. "I told him that I had, and Michael maintained that if things didn't change, the city was going to be like the Book of Revelation. We are going to be judged by God." Marc assured him, he'd spent a lot of time talking to pastors in the city and no one had ever said that to him, but he agreed. He asked him if he'd be willing to come and tell that to Eastbrook. Michael agreed. He said he'd never talked to a white church before. He knew people thought he was such a disturbing person, even the city was embarrassed by him.

Michael had gone on shows all across the country, saying he was going to burn Milwaukee down if he didn't see any change. He had already set tires on fire on freeway ramps; his threats had teeth to them, and people were really nervous. Marc didn't tell people at church that he'd gone to meet with Michael and invited him to come and speak. He just told the church he had invited a friend to come and talk, but he asked that nobody bring any guests that day. So, the following week, as Marc stood up to preach, down the aisle came Michael McGee with his wife and his bodyguard, quite obviously armed. They took a seat in the front row. At the end of the service, Marc dismissed nonmembers and asked that the doors be shut. He then told them he had invited

Michael McGee to come and speak, and the meeting was just for church members.

There were a lot of surprised looks. Half of the leadership wanted to get rid of Marc by that point. But before anyone could say anything, Michael went up to Marc and told him that he wasn't prepared. He didn't think Marc would ever actually let him speak. Marc told him to just relax and tell his story. Michael had never done that, but he got up and before he knew it, he had talked for about forty-five minutes. He told the church that he'd been raised in the city and loved the city. He went off to Vietnam and came back honorably discharged. But the problems in the city were so bad that he had to find a way to get people's attention. So he helped write a bill to the Assembly and Common Council to get ten million dollars set aside so he and the police chief could address some of the problems that needed to be addressed in the city. He was trying to work within the system.

In the midst of it all that Sunday, two black sisters and former drug addicts stood up and said, "Michael, it's Jesus! It's Jesus that can make the difference! Jesus is the hope of the city!" The two ladies were screaming out the words and repeating, only Jesus could make the difference. It was a wonderful moment. When Michael was finished speaking, Marc stood and said that he'd been to some of these City Council meetings and found them really frustrating too. They never accomplished the things that really needed to be done. What the church needed to do that day was to respond to Michael. Michael had been honest with the church members. Marc told everyone there that he'd like them to stand up, and by standing up, they would express their repentance for any prejudices they had and anything they may have done to hurt the black community in Milwaukee. This would be their chance. The whole church stood up. Michael came over to the microphone and put his arms around Marc and told him he loved him. Then he turned around and told everybody, "And if I've offended anyone here, please forgive me."

"That was the Holy Spirit upon him," Marc said. "Then the men in the church stood and lined up to talk to Michael. Some confessed that they had hated him for five years, others said for ten, then they started to cry and asked Michael to forgive them. Many men stood up and asked his forgiveness. That's when the Holy Spirit fell on our church and we became a city church, fear left. We certainly weren't afraid of Michael."

Marc found out afterwards that Michael was funded by the Black Muslims, and when they found out what happened that day, they changed all his telephone numbers so Marc couldn't call him. Marc went over to his house with a bunch of apple pies for his family. But he wasn't there, so he just left the pies. The Black Muslims wouldn't let Marc get near him again. But when all his Black pastor friends found out what he had done, their estimate of Eastbrook Church went off the map. He never talked to Michael again before his death. He never did get reelected. He lost his aldermanic position and became bitter. "But he changed our church."

"I never sat in church with someone with a big gun obviously sticking out from their backs before," Nancy said.

"If you're going to lead in Christ's name, you need to have that kind of opportunity," Marc said. "God makes changes in the church, but he doesn't do it all at once. This was one of those times. We had moved into the city, yet the city wasn't coming to us. People may get angry with you. You may have all this religious pride, like the Apostle Peter saying, 'I have never eaten anything unclean.' And God said, 'Don't call unclean what I call clean.' None of us are clean. We couldn't just say, 'Have you heard him on the radio...?' and leave it at that. Michael McGee connected us, and our meeting that day changed the future of Eastbrook."

Following that experience, Marc was invited to speak on missions at a Baptist Church Missions Conference in Rochester, Minnesota. During the first service, "everyone fell asleep." During the second service, Marc decided to tell them the story of Michael McGee. At that time, there had been a great influx of Somalis in Rochester. The city was struggling with how to handle the situation, and they asked Marc what he would do. "Invite them in, get to know them, and love them," was his response. And they listened. He had gained credibility through his story of Michael.

Marc was later invited to speak at the Christian Medical and Dental Conferences in Kenya and Thailand. It was quite an honor for Marc. Continuing education courses were combined with spiritual classes and Bible studies taught by well-known theologians. Marc went to teach week-long Bible Studies in both countries, offering a message of hope. Missionaries might find themselves in "the horror of great darkness." You can't do it alone, he would say. "Get up and walk with the Lord. Maybe you're not a preacher, but you have a great message to tell. And God will go before you and open doors if you are willing. In the end, it's all about our hearts."

CHAPTER 32

What God Builds In

"We see the evidence (of this) all around us, in so many
enterprises which years ago came into being under
the inspiration of Spirit-filled men of God, but which
organizationally have slowly outgrown their spiritual
content, until nothing of spiritual life remains, and
God is no longer consulted in their counsels—but
they do not live. Of these, as of the church in Sardis,
God would say, 'I know your record and what you are
doing; you are supposed to be alive, but (in reality) you
are dead.'" (Revelations 3:1, ANT)
— Major W. Ian Thomas

Milwaukee, Late 1990s

Marc never knew what a day would bring. He was just
waiting on the Holy Spirit. He knew how difficult that
was to explain to someone who didn't understand or hadn't
experienced it in their own life. He invited Ray Bakke
from Northern Seminary in Chicago to come and speak to
Eastbrook. When Ray asked Marc what was going to happen
at their Saturday evening service, Marc told him that he had
no idea. Ray was taken aback. Marc told him that he, Ray,

was going to talk, Dolores Wenzler, who oversaw the worship, was going to do the music. The Holy Spirit was there and Ray should watch Him work. At the end of his visit, he told Marc he wanted to talk to his staff. Ray politely told the staff that their pastor didn't do anything. "He just waits on the Holy Spirit and is meeting people all over the city. This is the most exciting thing I've ever seen. But I want to come back a year from now and see if you're still around!"

Marc would send people down to Trinity Seminary in Illinois for training if they wanted to preach. They would come back and tell Marc that according to their preaching course, he was doing everything wrong. There were about fifteen things they had learned you can do wrong when you're preaching and Marc did them all. But they were also told that there were some people who could get away with that, and Marc was one of them.

During this same period, Marc invited the Dean of Students from Trinity Seminary, Perry Downs, to come speak for a Family Ministry weekend at Eastbrook. They had all heard great things about him and were looking forward to his coming. He arrived at the Erickson house on Friday afternoon, and they had special meetings set up all weekend. Nancy got a call the night before he arrived from their son Paul's wife, Kyla, letting them know they were headed to the hospital for the delivery of their second child. Kyla asked if Nancy could watch Andrew, their thirteen-month-old, for the weekend. Nancy agreed. She had taught that morning, picked up Andrew, visited Kyla in the hospital, and stopped at the mall to pick up a pair of glasses.

She had Andrew in the car seat along with a girl from Poland, Teresa, who was staying with them. She got to the mall, parked, and left Andrew in the car seat with Teresa, thinking she would just run in, get the glasses, and quickly return. But when she came out, the car wasn't there. She didn't think the girl would take Andrew anywhere, but she started to get a panicky feeling. She walked all around and then went back into the mall and found a security guard. When she told him her car had disappeared, he stayed calm and offered to help. He asked what department she had walked through when she came in. And she remembered, through the lingerie. He told her she had gone out the wrong door. He walked her around to the lingerie door exit, and there the car was with Teresa and the baby sitting there. She thought she might have lost her mind, but she didn't lose the baby! Then Marc called to tell her he had an emergency call to make. He said to hurry home to care for Perry Downs and get him to church on time. She raced across town wanting to be a good host; time was getting away from her.

Perry was very gracious while Nancy was thinking about what she could do to whip up a quick dinner. Everything was frozen. Her mind was running through possibilities when she remembered the Friday fish fries Milwaukee is well known for. She asked him if he'd like to go for a fish fry with her, and he said, "Sure." They were supposed to meet Marc on the Eastside at the Eastbrook Center for the evening meeting at six-thirty p.m. She was wondering where she could take a thirteen-month-old baby. They drove to one place that was closed. The next place had a long wait. Finally, they were running out of time and options, so she asked him if it was okay if they went to a McDonald's drive-through. He laughed and said that was fine. His first bite spilled mayonnaise all over his tie. She told him he wouldn't need a tie for the evening anyway, but she was feeling horrible.

The first meeting of the family conference that night went well.

Nancy had invited thirty women over for coffee to meet Perry the next morning. She put out quite a spread, and just as he was beginning to talk to the ladies, Kyla and Paul walked in with the new baby. There was no sneaking in because they had an open-concept house, and pretty soon the baby was crying. To Nancy, it felt like chaos everywhere. With a new baby in the room to be oooh'd and aaah'd over and a thirteen-month-old to be awakened and dressed and everyone out the door, it seemed a major disruption in Perry's sharing. Flustered, Nancy just wanted to hide. But this was the way it always was.

That evening, there was another session for the Family Ministry Weekend. After Perry had preached, there was a man attending who was a teacher in the Milwaukee Public Schools, who was blind and dying of AIDS. Marc told Perry he needed to walk him home. So Perry insisted on walking along. They walked in the rain for about a mile to the man's home. On the way, this man told Perry, if he had heard this message twenty years before, he would not be dying of AIDS.

This so touched Perry Down's heart. He later told Marc that he had bought a new outfit to come to speak at Eastbrook. Now his tie was wrecked, his coat and shoes were wrecked, but he still felt so blessed because this man had come to Christ. Perry knew that God had used him.

"But you know what Perry Downs told the class he taught after all that?" Marc said. "If he could trade jobs, he would take a job as a custodian at Eastbrook Church. He said he loved our church that much. If we could offer him a place on our staff, he would take it." It wasn't the first time Marc had heard that. Some said they would come and run the sound system if they could just come and be at Eastbrook. There was nothing normal about the church.

Growing up in her Presbyterian Church in south Minneapolis where everybody sat in the same pew, everybody knew exactly when to stand and when to sit, everybody knew the service started with the Doxology and ended with Gloria Patri, everything Nancy experienced was predictable. And nothing was ever predictable at Eastbrook. She couldn't go back to the old mold if she wanted to. It was a wild life, but she was just along for the ride.

CHAPTER 33

Becoming Family

"Be joyful always; pray continually; give thanks in all
circumstances, for this is God's will for you in Christ
Jesus. Do not put out the Spirit's fire."
(1 Thessalonians 5:16-19, NIV)
Marc and Nancy's Life Verse

Late 1990s Continued

Throughout their ministry, watching Christians in places like Somalia and China, India, Egypt, and Syria, Lebanon and Jordan, Gaza, the West Bank, and Jerusalem, Marc and Nancy have come to know amazing people. Their job has always been to encourage and learn from them. "When I preached in any of these places, my message often began, 'What I'm going to say to you is what you already know and are doing.' They were boldly living out the Gospel in enemy territory."

These people are their models, those who live where it's not easy to be a Christian. "They know what it is to count the cost and choose Christ. They needed to hear about the strength we saw in them. Christian Arabs suffer particularly," Marc continued. "People assume all Arabs are Muslim. It's not true. There is an ancient Arab Christian Church in the Middle East. The important thing I can offer is friendship. I can do that. I may not be a great theologian or a great communicator, but I can be their friend. And they really want that. That's what the Indian-Christians want and the Chinese. They want a friend. When you become a friend cross-culturally, everything flows through that. It's amazing. We need to start every friendship with respect and listening."

Marc has a friend named Victor in the Middle East who is one of five sons. His father was a well-known pastor. Victor moved to London to escape Christ and went on to become a very successful businessman, but it didn't buy him happiness. His marriage was in trouble. That brought Victor back to the Lord and to Jordan where he and Marc became friends. Victor was a United Nations translator. Billy Graham later recruited him to do simultaneous Arabic translations at his crusades into the Middle East. God was beginning to use him. Marc received a call from Victor one day letting him know that he was in Minneapolis. He had finished all his work early and wanted to know if he could come and stay with the Ericksons. Marc was surprised. But he knew they had become true brothers when Victor asked if he could come.

"Victor told me that when he got up to preach one day in North Africa, something happened to him. The Holy Spirit came on him and he invited people to come forward. He was not a charismatic person, but people started speaking in tongues, and there were healings right there before his very eyes. God poured His Spirit into him."

When Saddam Hussein moved in and took over Kuwait, American troops were sent in to stop him. Marc wrote a letter to his friend Lucien in Lebanon, assuring him of their prayers, particularly for the Christians in Saddam's Army that were put in harm's way. Lucien told Marc that he was one of the only Americans who had written expressing prayer for the Christian minority in the Middle East when the Gulf War ended. American mission leaders had invited Lucien, Victor, and others to Atlanta to strategize new opportunities because of the "American Victory."

There was to be a prayer retreat for a small group called the Arab World Servant's Fellowship. Lucien and Victor invited Marc and Nancy to come to Lebanon. At the time, the U.S. State Department had banned Americans from travel to Lebanon at that time. The country was still in civil war. Marc asked Lucien if he could give him an official invitation. If so, he would risk it to be with the suffering church. They were issued the invitation from the head of a large Christian family in the Orthodox Church in Lebanon. Marc and Nancy decided to go. Marc was instructed not to let the officials stamp their passports on entry, or they could face a U.S. fine of $10,000 or be sent to jail. "Nan and I flew into Beirut, and I told her this as we were landing."

Thinking of their five children at home, Nancy asked, "When were you planning on telling me this?" In the near-empty airport, they went through security in Beirut and had the letter of invitation ready. The Lebanese man raised his arm, stamped the letter saying, 'Welcome to Lebanon.' Their passports were still clean. God had miraculously opened another door.

Syria was in control of Lebanon. "We couldn't tell the difference between Syrians and Lebanese," Nancy said as she recalled the night. "We walked past security, out into the blackness, wondering if someone would meet us." Lucien surprised them in the dark and walked them quietly to the perimeter of the airport parking lot. They got into a beat-up car full of bullet holes. "As we drove, we saw that the entire downtown city of Beirut was completely destroyed. Lucien explained that there were five Hezbollah checkpoints to go through between the airport and their home. We shouldn't speak, just pray."

It was a long ride to Lucien's home past those Hezbollah checkpoints. Soldiers with machine guns pointing through the car windows added to the drama. They always asked Lucien for his papers, but they didn't seem to notice Marc and Nancy in the back seat. "On arrival, we met Lucien's lovely Swiss wife, Hugette. Their home had been hit by artillery shells for the fourth time that day. The big windows overlooking the Mediterranean were boarded up, there was shattered glass all over the floor, and gunshot holes throughout their furniture." While helping to clean up the mess that night, they became family. And in the midst of it all came a knock at the door. Brother Andrew of Open Doors had come just to encourage the Accad's after hearing of yet another attack. The next morning, they went on up the mountain together to a Catholic Retreat Center where they met with key Christian leaders in the Middle East for the entire next week.

Brother Andrew was a famous evangelist that started Open

Doors in the Netherlands. He wanted to make a Christmas dinner for the Hamas Leadership in Lebanon during the civil war there because God said to love our enemies. So Eastbrook raised twenty-five hundred dollars for that dinner. Brother Andrew went and ate with them and shared the Gospel. After meeting with him in Lebanon, Marc asked him to come to speak at Eastbrook. Andrew's first response was, "Yes, how can we wake up the sleeping church in America?"

When Marc followed up with Open Doors, he was told that Brother Andrew was scheduled five years out, but he had a few days in the middle of one particular week he might possibly be able to come. Brother Andrew told Marc he would come. Then Marc let Andrew's staff know that he wanted him to stay at their house. They told Marc that Brother Andrew never does that. Marc said to ask him. "Andrew came and he stayed with us."

Years earlier, Brother Andrew had heard that the underground believers in China were desperate for copies of the Word of God, and needed to know they had not been forgotten. Mao had destroyed all the Bibles in China, and Brother Andrew knew God had called him to get Bibles into China and Russia. Destroying the Bibles hadn't destroyed the hunger in the hearts of Chinese Christians for the Word of God. They wanted Bibles. Brother Andrew took on himself the job of raising money to bring one million Bibles printed in Chinese to be distributed in China. He had to raise the funds without telling anyone what it was for. Without Chinese authorities being aware of it, he hired two barges and tugboats to bring the Bibles to a prearranged beach one night, and asked the church to coordinate ten thousand Chinese believers and couriers, to secretly meet him on that beach, to unload and distribute the Bibles. It all happened in one night. "With God nothing is impossible!" Nancy said.

~

Today, the Chaldean Church in Mosul has been wiped out in northern Iraq. People had to run for their lives when ISIS came. One of the oldest churches in the world is gone. Every church has been destroyed. Every Christian business has been taken over by ISIS. "Nobody knows where these people are. Most of them are probably dead," Marc said. "So what I believe about suffering is not theory. It's already happening. A hundred years ago, three million Armenian Christians were put to death. Seven-hundred-fifty-thousand Assyrian Christians were killed at the same time. Today, the suffering of Christians is severe in North Korea, Somalia, India, Russia, China, Nigeria, Syria, Sudan, and in so much of the world. The freedom that the American Church has experienced is not the norm in the world today. These people have really suffered. America is ripe for God's judgement."

"The turn to godlessness in our culture should be a warning that America's judgement is coming," Nancy said. "The day of the church being a spectator sport has come to an end. We can't afford to be connoisseurs of preachers, worship leaders, comfort, and beauty. The church is every believer. We all have to have a voice, take up our crosses, and let God lead. Our lives have simply been about building friendships, sharing what we have, opening up our home for hospitality, and not being afraid."

"We just became friends," Marc said. "If you want to be something among the Arabs, you have to be their brother and sister. They want to know we are family together in Jesus; they are our brothers and sisters through and through."

"We put our feet under the table with the same Father. We learned how big God's family is. We have to become one; no one is more or less than another. We came vulnerable, but they showed us how to count the cost again and again," Nancy added.

"What God is doing has very little to do with being a great preacher or great leader, having great resources or great ideas," Marc continued. "It has to do with really simple things like friendship. When trust is established, preaching can follow. When we think of China and Somalia, India and all these places God has introduced us to, I think of our friends."

"These people we met over the years, we introduced to Eastbrook, and they became a part of us. They became a part of our ministry, and we became a part of theirs. We truly have continued the relationships over the years. They are still family today, even though we live in different parts of the world," Nancy said.

CHAPTER 34

Risks and Miracles

*"I learned that courage was not the absence of fear but
the triumph over it. The brave man is not he who does
not feel afraid but he who conquers that fear."*
— *Nelson Mandela*

Somalia, 2000-2010

Over the next decade, twenty people from Eastbrook
served in Somalia. Their witness to Jesus held strong and true.
They won the hearts of the villagers in Bulo Burte. However,
the Islamists were not happy. One day a man stood up in a
mosque in Mogadishu and said that Eastbrook had "outraged
Islam" and the team should be killed. They incensed the
congregation with lies, until they dismissed them in a demonic
rage to go to destroy Eastbrook's headquarters. When the
angry mob arrived, the Ziebarth family with their three
children hid in a bedroom praying. They could see people
going by the windows, smashing and destroying everything
in sight. Yet the Islamists never entered that room. God
protected them. It was as if the fighters couldn't see the door
or windows. After that first rampage, the crowd left, but then
a second wave of zealots came from another mosque. When

they left, Darrell Ziebarth took his wife, Debbie, and three children and fled across the street to a U.S. AID home. But unfortunately no one was home. He quickly hid his family in the yard and snuck back into Eastbrook's headquarters to see if he could retrieve their documents from the small safe in the house. He was shocked to see the door of the safe torn off, but there in plain sight was a stack of U.S. passports and a stack of hundred-dollar bills untouched!

"Again, only God," Nancy said, recalling the story. The man who had called for 'Jihad' in Mogadishu against Eastbrook went on up-country to Bulo Burte. Again, he went to the mosque there, but he couldn't get the response he did in Mogadishu. There, in Bulo Burte, the leaders of the mosque knew the Eastbrook team. The Jihadists didn't realize Eastbrook had rebuilt the water system for the mosque so they could wash before they worshipped. Everyone in that mosque was friends of Eastbrook. Instead, the residents of Bulo Burte threw the Jihadists in jail and said to the team, "We're going to put you all in one house tonight and camp around you. If anybody comes to kill you, they're going to have to kill us first."

"When God is for you, who can be against you?" Nancy said.

Ahmed was subpoenaed to testify at a trial for a missionary before their Supreme Court. They told him to put his hand on the Quran and swear. But he said that he would not swear on the Quran. All the leadership of the country was there confronting him and asked why he wouldn't? Ahmed told them he was a Christian and followed Christ. Most Somali believers were secret believers, not Ahmed. Everyone thought that would seal Ahmed's death sentence, that they would take him out and shoot him right then and there. That's what Ahmed thought too, but instead, the judge asked him if he would tell the truth. Ahmed said that he would. The judge answered, that was good enough for him. So he had just basically said it was okay to be a Christian in Somalia. "I don't know how far that rippled down. In the past, almost everyone who became a Christian was martyred. They all knew a long list of people that had become Christians and were killed. It was high stakes. The fear at that time was real. But somehow God kept us from becoming frightened and we survived. That's why Nan and I had originally warned Ahmed and his friend as teenagers when they first came to our house to tell us they wanted to become Christians. We had told them if they were coming for any ulterior motives, it wouldn't be worth it to them. They wouldn't get God, and in addition, they would be persecuted. We wanted them to know we weren't going to give them money, we weren't going to get them to America. All we had to offer was God. But isn't God everything, the Pearl of great price?"

When Ahmed's family found out that he had become a Christian, they called a family meeting. His father told everyone that Ahmed had become a gaul (an unbeliever). He was going to have to leave the family immediately. He would deny Ahmed was his son, and he would no longer pay for his education. But the seven brothers defended Ahmed. They said he was a Somali and should be able to decide for himself what he wanted to believe.

So his brothers stood up for him. His oldest brother, Mohammad, was a pharmacist in Mogadishu and said he could come live with him; he would pay for his school expenses. Years later, Ahmed was reconciled to his father and mother, and Marc thinks they both became believers. Ahmed grew stronger through everything he suffered. He married Martha, and they had three children. He served the Lord faithfully among Somalis for twenty more years. They eventually moved to Nairobi to work with Somalis there. They both taught at Daystar University.

Ahmed's life was often threatened. God had kept him alive at least twice—first, he faced death with malaria in Bulo Burte during his early teens. At that time, his family took him to the SIM hospital, where Joy Newcomb took care of him. Later, he was at a Peace Meeting where clan leaders came to talk to the other clan leaders. The only person in the room that wasn't afraid was Ahmed. He kept asking the leader really pointed questions. One clan leader who wanted to take over ordered Ahmed killed. That clan later came with a grenade launcher, but just as they fired it, Ahmed shifted, so it missed his body, but it took off his leg. When his family heard about it and came to his side, they all began to cry. Ahmed told them to go find his leg. He was an American citizen and he always kept his passport in his boot. They found his leg and passport. He knew he needed emergency medical care, but didn't want to be operated on in Africa. He wanted to come to Milwaukee for surgery.

"The Red Cross flew him out of Mogadishu via Nairobi to Milwaukee, and before we knew it, he arrived here. It was a miracle." Marc's surgeon friend, Bill Dicus, went in to see him and told Marc that Ahmed had necrotizing fasciitis (a flesh-eating virus). He didn't know if they could save his leg. The procedure involved cutting off the dead flesh until the infection could be stopped. Day by day, they had to cut off more. Finally, they had taken his leg up to his hip, and it looked as if it was going to take his life. Marc went to him that night and told him the wound was not healing properly. If they couldn't stop it, he was going to die. Ahmed told Marc it was okay. He had told the Lord that he just wanted to see his wife and kids and Marc. He wasn't afraid to die. He had been able to do so much in his life that he was ready.

The following morning, Marc was at the men's ministry where a Lebanese man named Philipe Accad told Marc he had to talk to him. As it happened, Marc had just been to Manila, Philippines, for a Lausanne Conference and mentioned in his message at church that morning that he had heard a great speaker named Lucien Accad while he was there. After the service, Philipe introduced himself to Marc as Lucien's brother. This was his first time at Eastbrook. Philipe's and Lucien's father was a well-known evangelist in the Middle East under the Bible Society in Beirut. Lucien had taken his father's place in ministry. Philipe was a chef and referred to himself as "the black sheep of the family". He had married an American and moved to Milwaukee and recently returned to his faith. His story opened a wonderful, rich relationship between Eastbrook and the Accad family, and the church in the Middle East.

Philipe went on for about an hour explaining all this, and finally shared that he had received a Word from God that Ahmed was going to be healed. Marc couldn't believe he had talked so long before telling him that. They got in the car and drove to the hospital. In Ahmed's room, Marc told Philipe to tell Ahmed what the Lord had said to him. He said, "Ahmed, the Lord told me this morning that He is going to heal you, and you are still going to be a missionary to Somalia."

Marc talked to Bill Dicus, who whisked him back to the operating room, removed the dressings, and sure enough, the fasciitis was all gone. God had healed Ahmed, so he, Martha, and their children—sons, Afrah and Gedi, and daughter, Sophia—went back to work with Somalis, once again, in Nairobi. His life belonged to Christ. He was never afraid to die. He was later diagnosed with cancer, and they moved back to Milwaukee.

Ahmed's care was heavy for Martha to bear alone. They moved to the Erickson's home. While there, David and Grace Schenk came to write Ahmed's story, *Tea Time in Mogadishu*. Afrah and Gedi moved to the Erickson's daughter, Heidi's, house in the same neighborhood. Heidi and her husband, Dan Quinn, already had eight children, but Afrah and Gedi became numbers nine and ten. They were good brothers to the seven Quinn sisters and their brother. With the help of the Mennonites and Eastbrook, Ahmed was able to buy a house for Martha and his three children.

A few weeks before Ahmed died, Marc went to see him. Ahmed said, "Marc, you and I are famous. We've finally arrived. At a meeting of Somalis in London yesterday, El Shabbab put a 'fatwa' out on us, saying that we were dangerous, wanted men. They said, 'We had led ten percent of Somalia to Christ.' Oh, if that were only true! They probably would have killed us on sight, but they didn't have the correct pictures of us. They had pictures of someone else." It was prostate cancer that took Ahmed's life in his early fifties. When he finally breathed his last, the two families were there together. It was a holy time. When the undertaker came to pick up the body, they couldn't maneuver the gurney through the hallway. Marc had the privilege of carrying Ahmed's body in his arms to the waiting hearse. Marc felt the Holy Spirit remind him of when he first met Ahmed at just sixteen years of age. Now here he was carrying him. "It was the greatest privilege of my life. I knew Ahmed was no longer in that body. He was in heaven. We had such a good relationship. We were from such different cultures, but God put our hearts together as one."

One of Ahmed's greatest contributions, in addition to being a man of faith, a husband, and father of three amazing kids, was as a professor. Everyone wanted to be in the classes he taught. He taught Peace Studies at Daystar University in Nairobi. He was a scholar and said, in past centuries, Somalis were Christians. Some of the names of their ancestors were Christian names. "Their history is fascinating," Marc reflected. "I learned so much from Ahmed. I told him the first thing he was going to see after he died would be Jesus, but just past Him, he was going to see all the Somali believers that had gone before him. I didn't become a great doctor. I wasn't a great help running a hospital—that's not what God wanted me to do. What He wanted me to do was befriend Ahmed, and through him, begin to reach Somalia."

~

It's funny when you think about it," Nancy said. "Marc and I are both fairly shy people, and yet God has given us thousands of friends from all over the world. I think when we had people come from overseas, we never looked at them as celebrities and sent them off to a hotel. We treated them as relatives, as family. They stayed in our home, and we stayed in their homes. I guess that's different than what others might do. Looking back on all this, I don't know how it all worked out, but I know one of the keys in Christ's Kingdom is love. When you see churches get into trouble, it's when people stop loving each other. All our life, God just asked us to befriend people. We could do that."

"What we have to believe is that God just loves people," Marc said, echoing Nancy's words. "He wants us to know the joy of helping others find Him. As you understand more and more how He works, He'll do more and more in your life. He's working for us, and He's using circumstances to shape us and fit us into eternity, into a spot where we're destined to be. People are the coin of eternity. People are just so precious to God. You can't put enough value on them.

"After thirty years of leading the church to trust God to use all of us—at home, in the city, and around the world— God told me it was time to retire, to pass the baton to a new shepherd. God even chose His successor. Matt Erickson took over the helm for me at Eastbrook. I introduced him to all my friends. They trust him just like they trusted me. Of course, having Erickson for a last name didn't hurt."

CHAPTER 35

Two for the Road

"Anyone who intends to come with me has to let me lead. You're not in the driver's seat; I am. Don't run from suffering, embrace it. Follow me and I'll show you how."
(Matthew 16: 24, MSG)

Milwaukee, Wisconsin 2020-2023

One thing is for certain: the word "retirement" doesn't exist in either Marc or Nancy's vocabulary. As Nancy says, "As long as we have breath, Lord, use us!"

Closing Words for New Beginnings

Marc | Why Suffering?

I get up every morning and thank God for Parkinson's. I don't know why God allowed me to have it, but it has changed me. It has certainly humbled me. I have had to learn to walk, talk, and to keep learning. When Nan and I walk around our neighborhood, we see people all the time. They watch us, and I know they wonder how I am doing. But it gives me an opportunity to share my faith with them as I wouldn't have otherwise. I don't even have to say a word! I believe God is trying to show the whole church (universally) where it's headed and the important job we have to carry out.

We live in a world that is experiencing great suffering. People want answers, an explanation. If there is a God, why is there all this suffering? Suffering has great meaning. Some say God has lost control, or never had control, or doesn't even exist. Jesus left heaven and took on a human body for the very purpose of suffering and dying to redeem the fallen human race. Because of Jesus' suffering, the angels declared, " Worthy is the Lamb, to receive all power, wealth, wisdom, strength, honor, and praise." Jesus, the Lamb slain for us, is declared worthy to unseal the scroll of human history, making a place for us in eternity. Everything is predicated on who God is—alive and present with us today. Yahweh means I AM. He's not only in the past; He is here in the present. We don't really know who we are, but we know that when we see Him, we'll be like Him. He wants to remake us so that when He's done, we'll look just like Him. Not just a few of us. We're all going to look like Him. There are no unimportant people with God. He's going to fit us all together into one family, loving one another. Suffering can show us the limit of our own power and our need for Almighty God.

About six weeks before Jesus died on the Cross, He had a conversation with people at the temple. He said, Abraham rejoiced to see my day. They said, come on, you're telling us you're 950 years old? You've seen Abraham? And Jesus said, oh yes, before Abraham was born, I AM. He was there with Abraham and is still here with us—the great I AM, ever-present. He's seen all the shame and pain, all the heartache, and brokenness; He knows about it all. We move on. He's still there. The Cross sums it all up. If He didn't forsake His place in Glory and become flesh and blood in time, God wouldn't be able to reveal who He really is. He's the One who bears all the grief and all the pain. That's why the Cross is Good News for us. It shows how much God loves us.

And we're kind of stuck because when He comes to live within us, He'd like to live that kind of life, where He gets involved in all the pain and all the shame and all the heartache through us. We can actually identify with each other's needs, get our hands dirty, wash feet for the glory of God. This doesn't happen in many churches.

Usually, we hide behind masks pretending we are the good ones, we are successful, but that's not what God is looking for. He's looking for someone who admits their own brokenness and their need for a Savior, and is willing to get connected to others who are hurting. Jesus wants to forgive us and save us from lives of sin and guilt and shame.

Let me tell you one more story. My grandfather lived to be about seventy. I only saw him once. I don't remember what he looked like, but I heard stories about him all the time. He had stomach problems, ulcers, maybe even a bleeding ulcer. But one day when he was very ill, he went out to do his work, and the next thing he realized was that he was on the outside of heaven looking down on this huge, beautiful city. It was very bright, and God said, "You can come in if you want, or you can go out. It's up to you; you decide." And my grandfather said, "Well, my wife has ten kids. I'm not going to leave her alone with ten kids. I have to go back and help her." And the next thing he knew, he was in the living room, and the doctors were there giving him something to wake him up. He lived another ten or fifteen years.

He went all over North Dakota starting Sunday schools and distributing Christian education materials. There was a lot of fighting between the Catholics and Protestants, the Irish and Italian Catholics versus the Scotch and English Protestants. Prejudice ran deep. His church didn't want to have anything to do with the Catholics, but when my grandpa heard about it, he just went out the door, walked down to the Catholic Church, went in, and introduced himself to the priest. He told him that he knew people were saying unkind things about him, and it broke his heart. He asked him to walk through the city with him. He wanted them to link arms so the community could see them as friends.

So they walked, arm and arm—the pastor and the priest through the city from one end to the other. No one gave him any grief after that. That's the kind of guy he was. When my grandfather died, the priest wasn't allowed to go into the church for the funeral, so he stood outside until the end and there told everybody how much he loved their pastor. This was one hundred twenty years ago.

That's what happens when you've seen heaven. Prejudices just fall away. Divisions cease. We're all there in heaven! Just knowing that story really helped me when we returned to Milwaukee. I was about to meet a lot of different people. I'm now connected to all the denominations in the city. Now I'm just looking for brothers and sisters full of the Holy Spirit. All the denominations are my friends. That's a huge miracle.

It's all about the things God builds into us along the way. It's not our work that makes us worthy, it is the Worthy One, Jesus, who brings lasting value into our lives and into what we do. It's all about what God builds into us along the way. We may not know it, but we are all thirsty for God. That's why Jesus was crucified, to bring us back to God. He said, "It is finished." Death was turned to life, sin was forgiven, redemption was complete, Satan was defeated.

The Cross is the Tree of the Knowledge of Good and Evil. When man came to know evil, the Cross became a necessity. What does the Spirit say in Revelations 2:7? "He who has an ear, let him hear what the Spirit says to the churches. To him who overcomes, I will give the right to eat from the Tree of Life, which is in the paradise of God." This is the second tree. The angel guarded that tree from sinful man until the sacrifice for sin was made by Jesus.

There was no other way: Jesus, the perfect Son, had to become one with the human race. The verse that changed my life was 2 Corinthians 4:6. God, who said, "Let light shine out of darkness, made his light shine in our hearts to give us the light of the knowledge of the glory of God in the face of Christ."

When we're on our way to Heaven, and we get to the Great Assembly, we're going to overdose on stories. Can you imagine the stories we're going to hear? We're going to be agog with the glory of God's work in the human race. We've been around long enough to know that everybody's got stories, and we never get tired of hearing them. You can never write anybody off. There are no unimportant people.

If you're smart, you aren't keeping too busy. The competition of trying to be somebody who stands out interferes, and is totally inappropriate if you have God living in you. Being somebody means nothing. It's interesting that Jesus told all those who labor and are heavy-laden to come to Him and He will give them rest. I sincerely found Christ at age twenty-seven. Up until that time, I was working flat out to be the most committed Christian I could be. I believed in Jesus, I could make many things work. I could even preach to some degree. But when I found out I didn't have to live the Christian life in my own strength, I quit trying so hard. I never went back there.

I discovered it has nothing to do with me being something. It's all about Christ living in me. And the reason that that was really important to schizophrenics and people living in group homes with mental illnesses was because Christ could come and live in them too. So that puts us on equal footing. God is always getting us ready for eternity.

What we have to believe is that God just loves people, and He wants us to know the joy of helping others find Him. As you understand more and more how He works, He'll do more and more in your life. He's working for us, and He's using circumstances to shape us and fit us into eternity, into a spot where we're destined to be. People are the coin of eternity. People are just so precious to God. You can't put enough value on them.

Preachers can't do more than anybody else. They may think they can, but they can't. When it operates that way, the church will get smaller. When the darkness and persecution intensify, the church will be powerful if everyone is united and serving together.

Just remember, it's all about the Cross and sharing our testimonies, and not being afraid to die. It says in Revelation 12:11, they overcame "by the blood of the Lamb, and by word of their testimony; they did not love their lives so much as to shrink from death." The testimony, our experience, is not just knowing theology, but knowing God, and seeing how He helps us. It's a combination of the Cross, and our experience of Him—our testimonies—and having no fear of death that's going to take us through. It's all about the things God builds into our lives along the way.

Nancy | The Call of God

People may ask why we chose Ethiopia when we did, and Somalia just as the war broke out to do our early missionary work with young children in tow. I think meeting Dr. Linn McClenny the first year in med school was when we first heard that call. We both knew we were called to missions, but when we met Linn, who was the most humble, wonderful man, it was affirmed. He came to the University of Washington med school and shared with a group of Christians. When he finished, Marc said, "I want to work with him." And I thought, "Boy, I could work with him." He just had such a presence of God. From then on we started giving to his work and getting letters from him. That took a long time, through med school and through Marc's internship and through the Army. For about six years, we had the smallest token gift part of his ministry. So that was our goal. It was during that time, Marc also had the experience at Wheaton during a conference where he saw the picture of the Mosque overlooking the Indian Ocean, and he felt God said, "There." He came home and said, "I think we're going to Somalia." Dr. McClenny was a brilliant surgeon. People at the top so often become proud. Not Linn. There is a point in our lives when we must come to the end of ourselves. Pride has to be cut out.

It's a hard thing to answer for someone who doesn't know the Lord. It is a mystery, the call, and God is leading. When David said, "The Lord is my Shepherd," what did he mean? And how does God get us interested in something He wants to lead us into? The Bible starts there with Abraham, which is kind of a mind-blowing story when you think about it. Why would you walk out of civilization with God who is a Voice to you but not a tangible person? And what for? God didn't tell Abraham. He only said, "I'll show you the way, I'll go before you." That's the confidence God gives.

What did Sarah know about God that she would say to her husband, "Wherever you go, I'll go," and find God along the way? There was no discussion between Abraham and God, that we know, of Abraham asking, "Will I come back to Ur? Will I see this again?" How do you know? I think you have to find out for yourself if it is God calling. You ask if you have the ability to pull up stakes and follow. I think God equips who He calls, I know He does. And I think that He took away our fear, with the exception of our little struggle at Kennedy Airport over leaving seventy pounds of stuff behind. I don't think either of us had one night of struggle saying,

"God, where are we going? How will You provide? Will our kids be healthy and safe? Will you be there? What will we do?" We didn't know any of those things, but God made it all an adventure to say, "I'll be there, I'll go with you. And that was enough. We were wanting to be led, saying, "Shepherd, show us." And that's the best I can explain it.

I realized afresh today how big God is and how small we are. What makes us ever think we're so important that God can't do without us? Our contributions are small. As I go through the Psalms, I see that again and again. They always come back to the greatness of God, the Creator of the universe, far beyond our imagination and understanding. He can handle all our needs, but He gives us the privilege of being used by Him. With His help, we put one foot in front of the other, and step by step we begin to see Him, see His leading, His following, His surrounding us, and living in us.

We can't take on all the pain of the world, we can't take on all the problems. We have to trust. We just need to be available to be used. He'll use somebody else at the next point. I think this is one of the qualities I love so much in Marc. We never go anywhere where he thinks the people aren't worth bothering with. He always finds what God sees in them. I love that. And I would do it all again just to meet Ahmed Haile, or someone like him! A verse that just undoes me is 1 John 3:1, "How great is the love the Father has lavished on us, that we should be called children of God!" And that is what we are!

Forgiveness is big with God. He forgives our sins to make us forgiving people. We have to see through God's eyes and love deeply. We need people that speak faith into our lives. The world will not affirm our faith. It is not going to say, "Oh, those are wonderful people of faith!" The God of small things makes the world small and brings us together.

He always starts on the inside. We need to give up our pride and anger and forgive each other. We make it really hard for the Holy Spirit if we're not available to Him daily, let go of our unforgiveness, sin, and ego trips. This will help people believe forgiveness is available for them.

To me, being a Christian is about filling yourself in the morning with God's Word, praying, and then you watch. He brings people to you or takes you to them. You share what He has revealed to you, He gives you the words, He leads. Then that person shares it, and then the next, and the next, and on it goes. We must bear with one another in love. That's a Church. God using each person to be His hands and feet. We can't be spectators with a few stars. It has to be every one of us shining like stars in the darkness. We have to get our perspective right. We're just one little dot in the big picture of history. But we're aware God uses little dots.

Old age is the next challenge. How do we stay focused and growing when we no longer have a job or a schedule? When our bodies are weak and tire easily, when doctor's appointments fill our weeks? I was studying Revelations 2 (verses 1-7, NIV) last week. I was thinking of Jesus walking with us, His church. He knows us, the church universal and every local church, and even every single believer—we are each a temple of the Holy Spirit.

To the church in Ephesus, He commended them for

their good deeds, their hard work and perseverance, their separation from wickedness and their good theology. He noted that they had endured hardship for His name and not grown weary. But then the hard truth comes—they were still going through the motions, they'd lost their first love. I thought He was looking at me! Where are we just going through the motions? Have we lost our first love? We need to repent.

That night we went to bed. I prayed and was just dozing off when we heard a tremendous crash. It shook the house. We both sat bolt upright. Marc thought a plane had crashed in the neighborhood. I got up to look out. All the neighbors' lights had come on. As I checked through the house, I quickly realized our great majestic oak had given way and fallen on our house. An enormous limb and its branches had crashed into our guest room and bath. Neighbors gathered to make sure we were okay. The police and fire department arrived. They asked us to quickly pack what we needed and evacuate. We obeyed.

The next morning, we surveyed the mess. A tree expert came. He said that grand old red oak was three to four hundred years old, 58" in diameter. The outside was majestic, magnificent. It looked perfectly healthy, but it had rotted from the heart. So on that still quiet night, it finally fell.

I thought, God, that's Ephesus, that's America. I don't want that to become me. I want a heart that beats only for the Lord. He is the Potter. I am the clay. If He shapes my character, it will be beautiful. Why do we worry about all the externals—how we look, what we wear, comparing with others, when the only important thing is our heart for Jesus? Without Him, we will fall with a great crash!

He's a big God using our small things for His glory. It's not about us. We're just along for the ride. Everyone has a story to tell, so share yours boldly, for His glory!

Acknowledgements

"What then shall we say in response to these things. If God is for us, who can be against us?"

When I'm at a loss for words, I know there is one place I can always go for help. The Word. Sometimes it comes to me first, as if on wings, like right now. What could be better than Romans 8:31 to summarize the fearlessness and love that drive Marc and Nancy?

Thank you, Marc and Nancy, for the wonderful privilege of listening to your inspirational, heart-stirring, life-changing God Story. You continually remind us that it's not about us. It's not about what we do. It's not even about church or religion. Your lives show us that it's all about one Man, Jesus. And what happened when He followed the Will of His Father—the Way of the Cross—in humble obedience. Everything changed that day, and continues to, moment by moment, to this very day.

Your lives and the lives of those you have shared in the telling of your many adventurous experiences are models of humility. You show us how to be humble, to let go, and to ask for a spiritual surgery on our own hearts, so that our prayer can become like John the Baptist, saying, "More of you, Lord, less of me."

And how can it be that over all these years, since Pastor

237

Marc passed on the torch to Pastor Matt, it would be Matt's prayer before he preaches each Sunday? Only God could have orchestrated such a seamless transition from Marc and Nancy Erickson to Matt and Kelly Erickson. Thank you, Matt and Kelly, for continuing the story with a uniquely adventurous new chapter of God's love and resurrecting power during such a time as this.

God knew who would carry on the story before one of us came to be, just as He knows each of us by name and only wants the same from us—to know Jesus, and to call on His Name. When we do, we, too, can slide over, give Him the wheel, and prepare to become a part of something beyond what we could ever ask or imagine. Not to mention, be a part of the greatest Love Story ever told.

In a world that tells us to do more, to be more, to become more influential, more educated, more established, what our hearts need most today is a story such as Marc and Nancy's. They assure us that when we are rooted and established in God's love, less is more. As Jim Elliott summarized, we learn to "give what we can't keep to gain what we can't lose."

And now, to the Friday morning Women's Ministry and the ladies at Nancy's Table, to Lucy Storch for proofreading that early draft, and to my extended Eastbrook Church family, I offer my love and gratitude for your friendship and prayers.

To Michael T. Braun, Editor-in-Chief at Ten16 Press and his team, thank you for recognizing the value and importance of passing on stories like Marc and Nancy's for future generations to grab hold of. You are a joy to work with.

My gratitude also extends to Laurie Scheer, for her careful eye, guidance and encouragement, and to all my friends at Wisconsin Writers Association who have made a difference in this writer's life.

Finally, to my husband, Todd Farris, who was willing to sacrifice our time together so that I could write this book, to my son, Charlie, for the endless joy and inspiration he provides, to my late parents, Bill and Dee, my late brother Ed, my siblings John and Joan, and to all my family, may love be our everlasting legacy.

As Stuart Briscoe reminded me once when I most needed to hear it, it seems fitting to end this journey together looking to God—Father, Son, and Spirit—with hearts of praise: "Now to him who is able to do immeasurably more than all we ask or imagine, according to his power that is at work within us, to him be glory in the church and in Christ Jesus through all generations, for ever and ever! Amen." (Ephesians 3:20-21, NIV)

Chapter 13

i   Burton, Richard F., First Footsteps in East Africa; Or, an Exploration of Harar, 2011, page 9

ii Erickson, Delnora M., The Hand of the Potter, 1979, Chapter 1, pages 1–5

Chapter 17

iii Haile, Ahmed Ali, Shenck, David, Teatime in Mogadishu, 1987, page 34

iv Haile, Shenk, Teatime in Mogadishu, 1987, page 34

www.ingramcontent.com/pod-product-compliance
Lightning Source LLC
Chambersburg PA
CBHW051417090426
42737CB00014B/2706